"NEIL SIMON'S MOST DEEPLY FELT PLAY."
—UPI

Perhaps America's best-loved living playwright, NEIL SIMON was born on July 4, 1927, and grew up in Washington Heights, at the northern tip of Manhattan. He began his career in television as a writer on *The Phil Silvers Show* and Sid Caesar's *Your Show of Shows*. His first play was *Come Blow Your Horn*, followed by the musical *Little Me*. During the 1966–67 season, *Barefoot in the Park*, *The Odd Couple*, *Sweet Charity*, and *The Star-Spangled Girl* were all running simultaneously; in 1970–71, Broadway theatergoers had their choice of *Plaza Suite*, *Last of the Red Hot Lovers*, and *Promises, Promises*. Then came *The Gingerbread Lady*, *The Prisoner of Second Avenue*, *The Sunshine Boys*, *The Good Doctor*, *God's Favorite*, *California Suite*, *Chapter Two*, *They're Playing Our Song*, *I Ought to Be in Pictures*, *Fools*, and the acclaimed trilogy of *Brighton Beach Memoirs*, *Biloxi Blues*, and *Broadway Bound*. Mr. Simon has also written adaptations for many of his plays, transforming them into feature films. He lives in Bel Air, California, and has two daughters, Ellen and Nancy; a grandson, Andrew; and a stepdaughter, Bryn.

The Collected Plays of Neil Simon, Volumes I and II, and *Biloxi Blues* are available in Plume editions. *Brighton Beach Memoirs* is available in a Signet edition.

NEIL SIMON

A PLUME BOOK

Published by arrangement with Random House, Inc.

Ⓟ REGISTERED TRADEMARK—MARCA REGISTRADA

Library of Congress Cataloging-in-Publication Data

Simon, Neil.
    Broadway bound / Neil Simon.
        p.   cm.
    Third volume of the author's autobiographical trilogy of plays,
following Brighton Beach memoirs and Biloxi blues.
        ISBN 0-452-26148-1
        I. Title.
PS3537.I663B73   1988
812'.54—dc19   88-17044
                                                                                CIP

First Plume Printing, November, 1988

        3   4   5   6   7   8   9

PRINTED IN THE UNITED STATES OF AMERICA

For mv mother, father,
and brother

BROADWAY BOUND *by Neil Simon was first presented by Emanuel Azenberg at the Broadburst Theatre, New York City, on December 4, 1986, with the following cast:*

KATE	Linda Lavin
BEN	John Randolph
EUGENE	Jonathan Silverman
STAN	Jason Alexander
BLANCHE	Phyllis Newman
JACK	Philip Sterling

Radio Voices:

ANNOUNCER	Ed Herlihy
CHUBBY WATERS	MacIntyre Dixon
MRS. PITKIN	Marilyn Cooper

BROADWAY BOUND *was directed by Gene Saks. The setting was by David Mitchell, the lighting by Tharon Musser, the costumes by Joseph G. Aulisi, the sound by Tom Morse, and Peter Lawrence was the production stage manager.*

The year is 1949.

We are in the Jerome house in Brighton Beach, Brooklyn, New York—a working-class neighborhood about two blocks from the ocean.

It is a two-story frame house. On the first floor we see a living room and dining room, separated only by furniture. Stage right is the front door. Outside is a brick stoop and the surrounding houses. Just inside the door is a staircase that leads to the four upstairs bedrooms. In the living room area are a sofa, an armchair, and a console radio separating the two. Near the front door is a telephone.

In the dining room area is an old, beautiful dining table and five chairs. Just upstage of the table is a breakfront.

The furniture, curtains, wallpaper, and carpeting reflect the small portion of postwar prosperity which has come to the Jerome family.

Upstage center is a swinging door, which leads to the kitchen. Stage left and running up and downstage is a windowed porch. The kitchen is accessible either through the center door or from the dining room through the porch. A door from the porch leads to the backyard.

The second floor bedrooms are arranged as follows: JACK *and* KATE's *room is stage right, and* BEN's *room is stage left. Both are visible only when their doors are open. Fully visible and overhanging the living room are* EUGENE's *and* STANLEY's *rooms. Both rooms contain a single bed and a desk and chair.* EUGENE's *room is filled with books.*

All four bedrooms and the bathroom are connected by a central hallway.

It is about six P.M. *on a cold day in February. Snow covers the streets. It is already dark.*

KATE JEROME, *about fifty and graying, is wearing a sweater to ward off the chill that permeates the house. She is setting five places for dinner.*

As KATE *goes into the kitchen for more dishes,* BEN EP-

3

STEIN, KATE's *father, about seventy-five, comes out of his bedroom and starts slowly down the stairs. He is wearing a heavy cardigan sweater and carrying a brown paper bag. He is wearing his house slippers over his socks.*

KATE comes out of the kitchen as BEN *reaches the closet. She speaks louder to* BEN *than to anyone else.*

KATE   I didn't call you, Pop. It's not time for dinner yet.

BEN   Is it dinner yet?

KATE *(Setting out the flatware)*   In about a half hour. No one's home yet. Why don't you stay in your room? It's warmer in there.

BEN *(Taking his coat from the closet)*   Maybe I'll walk down to the store and get a cigar.

KATE   There's ice on the street, it's twelve degrees out. Eugene will get you a cigar when he gets home.

BEN   I like cold weather.

KATE   You're always complaining you're freezing.

BEN   I don't like it cold in the house. I like it outside. *(Putting on his hat)* I have nothing to read. Maybe I'll go to the library.

KATE *(Coming to* BEN*)*   It's six o'clock. The library is closed. Eugene has a million books upstairs.

BEN   I don't read what he reads.

KATE   He has everything.

BEN   He doesn't have a book about Trotsky.

KATE   You just finished a book about Trotsky.

BEN One book doesn't cover Trotsky. Thursdays they stay open till seven.

KATE This is Friday.

BEN I'll take a chance.
(He starts toward the front door)

KATE You want to fall and slip and break your hip again? You don't even have shoes on. You were going to walk in the snow in your slippers?

BEN *(Returning to the closet)* I'll put on my galoshes.

KATE What's in the brown paper bag?

BEN *(Sitting on the sofa to put on his galoshes)* Where?

KATE In your hand. What have you got there?

BEN Nothing. It's garbage. I was going to throw it away.

KATE Give it to me. I'll put it in the trash can.

BEN Will you stop treating me like a child. I'm your father, I'll do what I want. When I'm dead, you can treat me like a child.

KATE You're not going to the library. You were going someplace else. Where were you going?

BEN I'll go where I want! *(She grabs his galoshes and throws them into the closet)* If you don't like it, I'll move in with Blanche. Blanche treats me with respect. Don't interfere with me.
(BEN goes to the closet. KATE stops him at center)

KATE You never go out at six o'clock. Something is going on here. If there's something in that bag that's important, you tell me and I'll bring it there myself.

BEN The day I can't take care of my own things, they'll be praying for me at the synagogue. *(KATE grabs the bag from BEN)* Katey, don't!!

KATE *(Looking into the bag)* What is this? Is this your bed sheet? . . . Where were you taking it?

BEN To the Chinese laundry. They never close . . . I want it back, please.

KATE You soiled your sheet and you didn't want to tell me? Why? I've been washing your bed sheets since I'm ten years old . . . So you had an accident. It's all right, Poppa.

BEN At night I've had accidents. This is the first time during the day.

KATE So? What else have I got to do with my time? There's no one in this house anymore anyway . . . Take your coat off. You'll catch cold.
(She goes into the kitchen, taking the bag)

BEN *(Calling after her)* Not a word, you promise me? I couldn't stay here if the boys knew.

KATE *(From the kitchen)* The boys? Who sees the boys? I forgot what they look like.
(BEN sits on the sofa, still in his hat and coat. He puts his slippers back on and takes a newspaper from his coat pocket and reads.

EUGENE MORRIS JEROME comes running down the street, wearing a zip-up jacket with the collar up, and a scarf. He is twenty-three years old. He bursts through the front door and blows on his hands.

The front door is not locked. Don't forget, this is still only 1949)

EUGENE Oh my God! Hi, Grandpa! Did you hear? This is the coldest day in the history of the earth. Is

Stanley home yet? *(Crossing to the closet and yelling upstairs)* STAN???

BEN What are you yelling for? I hear you.

EUGENE *(Hanging up his coat)* I was yelling upstairs for Stanley . . . Why are you sitting in your coat?

BEN What?

EUGENE Why are you sitting in your coat?

BEN I was going out. Your mother changed my mind.

EUGENE *(Going to the dining table for an apple)* You're better off. It's freezing. I saw a man kissing his wife on the corner and they got stuck to each other. Mr. Jacobs, the tailor, is blowing hot steam on them.

BEN *(Looks at him, concerned)* Two people got stuck?

EUGENE If they can't get them apart, they're going to have to sew all their clothes together.

BEN They can't get them apart?

EUGENE *(Straddling a dining chair and facing BEN)* It was a joke, Grandpa.

BEN That was a joke? *(He rises and starts toward the closet)* What kind of joke?

EUGENE I made it up. It's not really a joke. It's just funny.

BEN To who?

EUGENE To me.

BEN So if it's funny to you, what are you telling it to *me* for?

> *(*BEN *goes to the closet and hangs up his coat, but leaves his hat on)*

EUGENE *(To audience)* The strange thing about my grandfather is, he has totally no sense of humor. None. But everything he says, I think is funny. Maybe because he doesn't mean it to be. If he tried to be funny, he wouldn't be. *(To BEN)* Where's Mom?

BEN What kind of animal wears a zipper?

EUGENE A zipper? I don't know. What kind?

BEN A horsefly.

EUGENE *(To audience)* See what I mean?

BEN *(Crossing back to the sofa)* That's a joke! Not two people got stuck together. You understand?

EUGENE Yes, Grandpa. Thanks for the priceless information. *(To audience)* My mother and father are the same way. I could say something so funny that the pictures on the wall would get cramps from laughing, but those three just stare at me like dead bodies. I'm trying to become a comedy writer someday, and this is the encouragement I get.

BEN What kind of fish sings an opera?

EUGENE What kind of fish sings an opera? . . . I give up. What kind?

BEN A halibut.

EUGENE A halibut?

BEN I got it wrong. I thought it was a halibut, but it doesn't sound right.

EUGENE *(To audience)* Okay? I guarantee you that a halibut is funnier than the real answer . . . I mean, look at him. Sitting there with a hat on. If he put it on to be funny, it would be dumb. But he doesn't know he's got it on, so it's hysterical.

BEN Does a mackerel sound right?

EUGENE Don't work on it, Grandpa. It'll come to you. *(To audience)* My brother, Stanley, is the only one who appreciates my humor. When I make Stanley laugh, I feel like Charles Lindbergh landing in Paris . . . And Stanley comes up with great ideas. That's why the two of us teamed up. We're going to be a comedy writing team . . . *(Like a radio announcer)* "The Jack Benny Show was brought to you by Lucky Strike and was written by Sam Perrin, Nate Monnister, Milt Josephsberg, and Stanley and Eugene M. Jerome."
(He hums "Love in Bloom" as KATE *comes in from the kitchen with dinner plates)*

KATE *(Circling the table, setting plates)* What are you eating an apple for? I made chocolate pudding.

EUGENE It's not a fatal combination, Mom. Where's Pop? I have to talk to everybody.

KATE I don't think he'll be home for dinner.

EUGENE Again? That's twice this week. So what are you setting his place for?

KATE The hell with him, that's what I'm setting his place for.
(She returns to the kitchen)

EUGENE *(Crossing to sit beside* BEN *on the sofa)* Grandpa? What's wrong with Mom? Did she and Pop have another fight?

BEN It's none of my business.

EUGENE You know what's going on. She talks to you. You can tell me.

BEN She *used* to talk to me. She doesn't talk to me anymore.

EUGENE She snaps at everybody now. Even Stanley can't get a rise from her . . .

BEN She was always like that. As a child, she could shut off for a month.

EUGENE I can't picture her as a girl. Was she really supposed to be such a good dancer?

BEN I only saw her dance once. I didn't like to go to those places. She used to win cups at the er . . . the er . . . that dance place.

EUGENE The Primrose Ballroom?

BEN At the er . . . that place near Long Beach.

EUGENE The Primrose?

BEN It was a big dance place in those days . . . the Primrose Ballroom!

EUGENE Right. *(To audience)* Even his timing was terrific . . . He was the greatest teacher of comedy I ever met . . . Only he didn't even know I was studying him.

BEN Sure, she was a terrific dancer.

EUGENE She told me once she danced with George Raft.

BEN Who?

EUGENE George Raft. The movie actor.

BEN I know who he is . . . Yeah, sure, she danced with him. He wasn't a star then. He was just a greasy-looking kid. He used to go around to all the different ballrooms and pick out the best dancer. She was fifteen, sixteen years old. Not pretty. She was never pretty. But she was graceful on her feet.

EUGENE   Why didn't she ever try to become a professional? Wasn't she good enough?

BEN *(Shrugs)*   She had the accident. She burned half the skin off her back. Twelve girls died in that fire. The owner of that shop went to jail. There was no ventilation, no back door. She couldn't walk for a year . . . She never went down to the beach again. Not with her back like that . . . Her sister Blanche was a beautiful girl. There were boys lined up outside the house just to look at her. But Blanche couldn't dance a note.

KATE *(Entering from kitchen with a pitcher of water and water glasses, which she puts on the sideboard)*   What are you two talking about?

EUGENE *(Crossing to KATE)*   About when you used to dance with George Raft.

KATE   You see? He still doesn't believe me, Pop.

EUGENE   Who said? I believe you. One day I'm going to write a movie starring George Raft, and he goes into this club, takes your hand, and dances a tango with you.

KATE   I did the fox-trot better. Make it a fox-trot.

BEN *(Crossing to the table)*   What was the name of that place where you danced?

KATE   The Primrose Ballroom.

BEN *(To EUGENE)*   That was it. The Primrose!

EUGENE   Okay. Listen, everybody. I have major news. This is serious.

KATE   Where's Stanley? The pot roast is almost dry.

EUGENE   Listen to me, will you? I have to talk to you.

KATE   Pop? You want a little wine tonight?

BEN   No wine for me. Too much acid. I'll have a beer.

KATE   We're out of beer.

BEN   You got wine?

EUGENE   *(To audience)*   If I could just get these two on television. *(To* KATE*)* Will you please come in here and sit down. I have spectacular news for this family.

KATE   *(Bringing in relishes from the kitchen)*   What family? You see a family in here?

EUGENE   Please sit. *(He seats* BEN *upstage of the table and* KATE *at the left end of the table)* Okay . . . ready? I wish to announce that your youngest son, Eugene Morris Jerome—is getting married.
   (A beat of silence)

BEN   A Jewish girl?

KATE   He's kidding, Pop. He's not even going with anyone, how's he getting married?

EUGENE   True! True! I am not going with her—yet! But I've seen her. Her name is Josie. I talked to her. I had lunch with her. I saw the color of her eyes. This is marriage, Mom. This is the girl for the rest of my life.

KATE   This is the same girl you met last summer?

EUGENE   No, no! I hate that girl. I never liked her.

KATE   You went with her for a whole summer.

EUGENE   I had nothing else to do. She was nice on the first date . . . *Part* of the first date. Until nine-thirty.

BEN   He liked a girl until nine-thirty?

KATE   He's kidding. That's a joke.

BEN   That's a joke, too? Ask him to tell you about the people who got stuck together.

EUGENE   This girl is serious. I knew it the minute I saw her. Her father owns a music company on the same floor where I work. She writes poetry. She paints. Her father hung her paintings all over his office. She's incredible. She plays tennis. She plays golf. She plays softball. She's been to Europe. She hums Bach and Beethoven, and she can whistle Rachmaninoff. She has jet black hair and olive skin, and when she walks down the street, construction workers fall into the cement. If I live to be a hundred, I'll never meet a girl like her again.

KATE   She likes you too?

EUGENE   *Likes* me? I took her to lunch, and we ate from the same chopsticks. We couldn't stop talking. Philosophy, literature, sports . . . Yeah, she likes me all right.

KATE   I never heard you so excited about a girl.

EUGENE   There's one minor complication, though. She's engaged to be married.

BEN   She's what?

KATE   He's kidding. It's another joke.

EUGENE   No. Really. She's engaged to a Harvard Law student. But I'm not worried. I think I have the inside track.

KATE *(Getting up and going into the kitchen)*   I have to check the pot roast.

EUGENE *(Calling into the kitchen after* KATE*)*   She's breaking it off. She's not in love with him. She told him, but he doesn't care. He wants to marry her anyway. That's how great she is. *(As* KATE *comes out of the kitchen with* BEN*'s wine)* If she was marrying him, would she have had lunch with me today?

BEN   Maybe she's looking for wedding gifts.

KATE *(Setting out napkins)*   She sounds fickle, if you ask me.

EUGENE   I want to bring her to dinner next week. I want her to meet the family.

KATE   It's been a long time since this family ate together.

EUGENE   On a Sunday. Everybody's home on Sunday. All right?

KATE   We'll see. Who knows what'll happen by then. I'm sure she's a nice girl, but eat from your own chopsticks.
   *(*KATE *returns to the kitchen.* EUGENE *crosses toward the stairs)*

EUGENE *(To* BEN*)*   She never turned down a chance to cook for someone before . . . Something's wrong between her and Pop, isn't there? *(Looks back at* BEN*)* Grandpa? Did you hear me? *(To audience)* He's sleeping. He's probably working on the halibut joke.

KATE *(Coming out of the kitchen and calling up after* EUGENE*)* Where are you going? We're eating soon.

EUGENE I'm not leaving the country.
(EUGENE *goes into his bedroom, turns on the light, and begins to write in his journal.*
KATE *returns to the kitchen.*
STANLEY JEROME *comes walking briskly down the street. He is twenty-eight, wearing a suit, tie, over-coat, and hat. He wipes his shoes carefully on the front mat, then enters the house. He is very excited)*

STAN *(Hanging his coat in the closet)* Grandpa? Is Eugene here? *(Screaming upstairs)* GENE!!

BEN *(Waking abruptly)* What the hell are you screaming for?

STAN I'm sorry. I didn't know you were sleeping.

BEN Then ask me. If you asked me, I would have told you.

KATE *(Entering from the kitchen)* You walk in the snow without rubbers? The pot roast is half dry. Tell Eugene it's dinner.

STAN We haven't got time, Mom. We'll take a sandwich later.

KATE What do you mean? No dinner?
(Upstairs, EUGENE *puts down his journal and comes downstairs)*

STAN We have to get right to work. *(Again, shouting upstairs)* GENE!!

KATE I've been cooking since two o'clock. Your father doesn't come home. You tell me no dinner. What am I, a slave here? . . . Sit down, Poppa! It's ready!

EUGENE *(At the foot of the stairs)*   What's up?

STAN *(To* EUGENE*)*   What are you doing now? Whatever you're doing, forget about it. Back upstairs.
We've got to start in right away. Mom, no calls for
us. Take a message, we'll get back to them. We may
be up all through the night, so don't get nervous if
you hear us yelling. *(To* EUGENE*)* Come on! Let's go.
We're wasting time.
   *(*STAN *starts to dash upstairs)*

EUGENE   You mind telling me what this is about?

STAN *(On the stairs)*   We got a job at CBS! The Columbia Broadcasting System.

EUGENE   *WHAT???*

STAN   I can't believe how much I did today. I was
running all over town. I met everybody. I mean, I
would make a terrific agent. I talked to these people
like they were my friends . . . I met Abe Burrows!
He said to me, "Good luck, kid." . . . *(To an uncom-
prehending* KATE *and* BEN*)* Abe Burrows, the greatest
comedy writer in the business . . . I was on the
executive floor, long hallway, pictures of every star
in the history of CBS—Jack Benny, Ed Sullivan,
Arthur Godfrey, Edward R. Murrow.

KATE   You met them?

STAN   No. Their pictures. *(To* EUGENE*)* There's too
much to tell. I haven't got time. We have to start
working. I'm so excited, I'm still shaking. Come on,
let's go!

EUGENE *(As* STAN *again starts up the stairs)*   Wait a minute! You mean the regular CBS?

STAN   No, the fake one!

KATE   Can't you talk this over at dinner?

STAN   Is that all you care about? Your dinner? The most important thing that's ever happened in our lives, and you're worried about a lousy pot roast?

KATE   *(Obviously hurt, she goes to the kitchen)*   Just like your father. You're getting to be just like your father every day. Next thing you'll turn Eugene against me, too.

STAN   I'm sorry! . . . Mom? Ah, shit! *(To EUGENE)* Come on.
        (EUGENE and STAN run upstairs as KATE comes charging out of the kitchen)

KATE   What did you say?

BEN   *(Ushering her back into the kitchen)*   He didn't mean anything.
        (EUGENE and STAN go into STAN's room. EUGENE sits in the chair. STAN takes off his jacket and tie)

EUGENE   All right, tell me slow. Tell me everything. What kind of a job did we get? When do we start? How much money do we get paid?

STAN   I didn't discuss details. If they like the sketch we bring in, then they'll hire us.

EUGENE   If they like the sketch, then they'll hire us? You mean it's not a job, it's an audition?

STAN   It's a job. They just have to like it first.

EUGENE   I knew it was too good to be true.

STAN   Let me take care of business. I got us the audition, didn't I?

EUGENE So it *is* an audition. Why can't you say so? I don't mind an audition, but you make it sound like we're leaving for Hollywood tomorrow.

STAN We discussed Hollywood. I said we would have no problem in moving to Hollywood. We could leave immediately, if they wanted.

EUGENE CBS asked if we wanted to go to Hollywood?

STAN No, I brought it up so they would know how we felt. You have to have confidence when you talk to these people . . . That's why I introduced myself to Abe Burrows.

EUGENE You introduced yourself?

STAN In the elevator. I said, "Mr. Burrows, the greatest thing that could ever happen to me is to work as a writer on your staff." And he said, "Good luck, kid." And got off on the twelfth floor.

EUGENE That's why he said—"Good luck"? You made it sound like you had lunch with him or something.

STAN Did *you* talk to Abe Burrows?

EUGENE That's not exactly talking to Abe Burrows. That's like the pope waving to you in the Vatican.

STAN You say hello to people like that three or four times in the elevator, and after a while they remember you. I'm starving. Do you have anything in your room? Some cookies or something?

EUGENE Why don't we have dinner first?

STAN We haven't got time for dinner. We have to work.

EUGENE If you can eat cookies, you can eat pot roast. It just takes another few minutes to chew it.

STAN (*Pulling* EUGENE *to his feet*) All right, go get a couple of sandwiches. We can eat here while we work. And some milk. And some dessert. A piece of cake, whatever we've got.

EUGENE (*At the door, turning to* STAN) How late are we going to work?

STAN (*Sitting in the chair, pads and pencils ready*) Until we finish. Maybe all night. They want it tomorrow morning at ten o'clock.

EUGENE They want a finished sketch by ten o'clock in the morning?

STAN That's how television works. They want it good, but they want it fast. Those shows are on every week, not twice a year.

EUGENE (*Sitting on the ottoman*) We never wrote a sketch in less than three weeks. And we only wrote one sketch . . . And we didn't even finish it . . . And the first part needs rewriting . . . Maybe we're not ready for CBS yet.

STAN You want me to call them up and tell them that? We'll never hear from them again . . . Once that kind of thing gets around, you're through at *all* the networks.

EUGENE You mean CBS is going to call NBC and ABC and tell them that two guys auditioning from Brighton Beach can't be depended on?

STAN Maybe. Do you want to take that chance?

EUGENE You actually believe that our names are going to come up in a meeting at ABC and NBC?

We're not even writers yet. You're the manager of boys' clothing at Abraham and Straus. I'm in the stock room of a music company. Our names don't even come up where we work.

STAN *(Standing)* What is it, Eugene? Are you afraid? If you're afraid, tell me. You have to have confidence in this world. If you don't have confidence, I'll *always* be in boys' clothing and you'll always be in the stock room.

EUGENE Why will *you* always be in boys' clothing if *I* have no confidence? Your career doesn't depend on my confidence.

STAN Yes. It does. We're a team. I need you; you need me. You have a great comic mind. I'm the best editor and idea man in the business.

EUGENE You really believe that?

STAN Absolutely. I have an eye for talent, and we have talent. When Joe DiMaggio came up from San Francisco, didn't I say he'd become one of the greatest ballplayers of all time?

EUGENE Because he was already a great ballplayer in San Francisco. Why are we so great? We sold three comedy monologues to a guy who plays weddings and bar mitzvahs.

STAN Right. And his salary has tripled in three months. Now all the young comics are starting to come to us. How do you think I got in to CBS? My friend Mort Garfield, the press agent, showed the monologues to the head of comedy development . . . Eugene, I'm going to get us everything we ever dreamed of. If you don't have faith in us, I have enough for both . . . Please trust me . . . Now go get the sandwiches. I want to start working on some ideas.

EUGENE   I didn't know we were going to work to-night.

STAN   Well, we are . . . Put some lettuce on my sand-wich. And mayonnaise.

EUGENE   The thing is, I wanted to see this girl to-night.

STAN   Well, now you won't see her. And get me some cucumbers.

EUGENE   I could leave by seven and be back by nine. I could write on the subway. I just have to see her.

STAN   You can see her another night. What's wrong with you?

EUGENE   She's engaged to a guy from Harvard. She wants to break it off, but he's coming in tomorrow to talk her back into it. If I don't convince her I'm the guy for her, he's liable to talk her into going through with it.

STAN   If he can talk her into it, what do you want her for?

EUGENE   Because she's perfect. And you only get one chance in your life of meeting a perfect girl.

STAN   You know how many perfect girls there are in Hollywood? They're *all* perfect. In two years you'll be *sick* of perfect girls. You'll be begging for a plain one.
    (EUGENE *goes to his own room and begins to dress for his date.* STAN *is in pursuit*)

EUGENE   An hour and a half, that's all I'll be gone. If I don't talk to her face to face, I'll lose her, Stan. I know it.

STAN   Eugene, as much confidence as I have in us, I don't have that much confidence that we can write the sketch by tonight. But we have to try. Remember the story Pop told us? How he had the opportunity to go into his own business with a friend . . . how he stayed up all night thinking about it . . . and he couldn't make up his mind. A week later it was too late. His friend lives on Park Avenue now, and Pop is still cutting raincoats . . . Maybe this is the only chance we'll ever get. Maybe not. But are you willing to risk everything for a girl you might not even be interested in by next week?

EUGENE   I'll be interested in her for the rest of my life.

STAN   Then go out with her. Take as much time as you want. I'll write the sketch myself. *(Storming back to his own room)* I mean it. I'm not going to blow this opportunity.

EUGENE   Never mind. I won't see her.

STAN   I said, I'll do it myself.

EUGENE *(Going downstairs)*   Don't do me any favors.
        (KATE *and* BEN *enter from the kitchen.* KATE *puts* BEN's *soup on the table. He sits down to eat)*

KATE *(To* EUGENE*)*   Are you eating or not?

EUGENE *(Going into the kitchen)*   We're having sandwiches upstairs, so NBC and ABC won't be mad at us.
        (KATE *follows* EUGENE *into the kitchen.*
            BLANCHE MORTON, KATE's *sister, comes down the street. She wears a mink coat and fur hat. She looks*

very prosperous. She rings the doorbell. No one an-
swers. BLANCHE *opens the door and walks in. She*
crosses into the dining room. We can sense some ten-
sion between BLANCHE *and* BEN)

BLANCHE   Hello, Poppa.

BEN *(Glancing up from his soup)*   Who's that? Blanche?
I didn't hear the limousine pull up.

BLANCHE   It's not a limousine, Poppa. It's just a plain
Cadillac.
(She kisses BEN. *He is clearly uncomfortable)*

BEN   Like John D. Rockefeller is just a plain business-
man.

BLANCHE *(Putting her purse and gloves on the sofa)*   It got
stuck in the snow, just like other cars. I had to walk
the last two blocks . . . Where's Kate?

BEN   What happened to the colored fella who drives
you around?

BLANCHE   Robert? He's still with us. He was calling a
garage to get us pulled out.

BEN   You pay him enough money, he could have car-
ried you here.

KATE *(Entering from kitchen)*   Why didn't you tell me
you were coming? I could have made extra dinner.

BEN *(To* KATE)   Why? Somebody's eating it besides
me?

BLANCHE   Thank you, Kate. I didn't come for dinner.
I wanted to talk to Poppa.

KATE   You had to come out in this weather? We have
a telephone now, too, you know.

(Everything seems to be an innuendo about the differences in their economic standing.
  EUGENE *enters from the kitchen)*

EUGENE *(Crossing down to* KATE*)* Mom, I'm having trouble with the pot roast.

KATE What did you do?

EUGENE Hello, Aunt Blanche.

BLANCHE Hello, Eugene.

EUGENE I didn't slice it right. I shredded it. It looks like shoelaces.

KATE I told you to let me do it. What do I bother cooking for?
  (KATE goes into the kitchen)

EUGENE *(To* BLANCHE*)* How's Nora?

BLANCHE She's fine. Her children are wonderful. She thinks the new baby looks just like you. He's going to be so handsome.

EUGENE Is that what she said? What did she name him?

BLANCHE Myron Isaac.

EUGENE Myron Isaac.

EUGENE *(To audience)* Myron Isaac Eisenberg. Poor kid. Wait till he tries to date a girl from Mount Holyoke.

KATE *(Shouting from kitchen)* EUGENE! WHAT DID YOU DO TO THIS MEAT??

EUGENE *(Going slowly into the kitchen)* I KILLED IT! IT WAS HIM OR ME, MA!! I KILLED THE POT ROAST!!

BLANCHE *(Waiting for* EUGENE *to disappear into the kitchen, and turning to* BEN) Momma is sick, Pop.

BEN That's a beautiful coat. What do you need a Cadillac for with a coat like that?

BLANCHE The doctor tells me if I don't move her to Florida, he can't guarantee what'll happen to her.

BEN I thought we had a bargain.

BLANCHE *(Sitting on the sofa)* Not talking about Momma is not a bargain, Poppa. It's a punishment. To me, to Momma, to the whole family. And I'm not leaving here tonight until we talk about her.

BEN *(Rising and crossing to* BLANCHE) Who's stopping you? Take her to Florida. She'll outlive the palm trees, believe me.

BLANCHE You can be so cruel sometimes.

BEN What did I say? I wished her a long life. You come here and aggravate me while I'm eating my dinner, and *I'm* cruel?

BLANCHE Do you know what she says to me at night? The very last thing before she goes to bed? She says to me, "Why does that man hate me so much?" What do I answer her, Poppa?

BEN *(Crossing to the armchair)* You don't. Because she'll ask it again tomorrow. Her whole day is built around why do I hate her so much. She sits on park benches and asks strange women why I hate her so much.

BLANCHE Why do you?

BEN Who said I did? *She* did, I never said it ... I have feelings for the woman, I always will ... But I can't

live her kind of life, she knows that. I hope she lives another fifty years, whether it's on Park Avenue or in Miami Beach. But these are my roots. I lived here most of my life, this is where I want to die.
(BEN *sits in the armchair*)

BLANCHE She's sick, Poppa. This is not the place for her. The cold wind coming off the ocean would kill her in two years. Thank God I can afford to send the both of you to a warm climate. It would make all of us so happy to see the both of you living together in comfort for the rest of your lives.

BEN Comfort doesn't make me happy. I don't need some place where it's hot twelve months of the year. April till October is all the sun God meant us to have. To want more is a crime against those who were born without. Read your Trotsky.

BLANCHE Don't turn this political, Poppa. This is *not* political.

BEN *Everything* is political. The soup in my dish is political. The bread on my plate is political. And the four thousand-dollar coat on your back is political. *(Rising and going back to his place at the dining table)* Don't tell me about things I was taught from the day I was born.

BLANCHE *(Rising)* Momma's health is *not* political. Momma's love for you is *not* political . . . When you can't find a reasonable answer for something, you always turn to Trotsky for help. *(She turns angrily away from* BEN*)*

BEN *(Crossing to the sofa)* You're angry with me because I won't live in your high-class apartment house where a year's rent could feed everyone on this block for a year? With a man in a uniform opening doors for me who's ten years older than I am? I'm not dead yet, I can still push a door open. Because I don't go to your fancy Park Avenue doctors four times a week? How much money did he get for telling your mother to move to Florida? I got friends who would have told her to move for nothing.

    (BEN *sits on the sofa*)

BLANCHE   And why are you so angry with me? Because you were brought up to despise the rich? I didn't marry Saul because he was rich. I'm so used to not spending money, he had to teach me how to do it. *(Coming to sit beside* BEN*)* But if he is loving enough to offer my parents the opportunity to live out their lives without worrying, for the first time in their lives, about where the rent was coming, what in God's name is wrong with it?

BEN *(Lowering his voice)*   I can't leave here. Not now.

BLANCHE   Not now? Then when?

BEN   Are you so blinded by your own life, you don't see what's happening to your sister's? Don't you know what's going on between her and Jack?

BLANCHE   No. What are you talking about?

BEN   He's getting ready to leave her. Tomorrow, next week, next month, who knows? He stays because he doesn't have the courage yet to go. But he's going, trust me.

BLANCHE   I don't believe that. Not Jack.

BEN   Not Jack, she says . . . A man gets older, he changes. He suddenly realizes he only has a few years left to do what he thought he had a lifetime to do.

BLANCHE   Jack loves Kate. He's always loved her.

BEN   Absolutely. But at fifty-five, he can overlook it.

BLANCHE   He depends on her. She manages his life.

BEN   Lucky for her. Otherwise, he would have left last year.

BLANCHE   Oh, God. Don't tell me this. It's the last thing I ever expected to hear.

BEN   Do you understand why I'm telling you I can't leave this house? Stanley and Eugene are grown men. Their life is just starting. It's time for them to leave this place. Do you know what it would be like for her to be alone? A woman who doesn't know a thing in this world except how to serve someone? If she can't make dinner for somebody, her life is over . . . You take your mother to Florida. You take care of her. But as long as I'm alive, I'll eat in this house.

EUGENE   (*Coming out of the kitchen with a tray of sandwiches*)   Your dinner will be ready in a second, Grandpa. Mom is sewing the pot roast back together.
   (EUGENE *starts up the stairs, stopping at the top*)

BLANCHE   Maybe Jack won't leave. Maybe they'll work things out.

BEN   Maybe . . . I'll stay here until maybe.

BLANCHE   I would do anything in the world for Kate. But I've got to take care of Momma first . . . If I bring her down to Florida, I can only stay a few weeks. I can't leave Saul to spend the winter in New York alone. She doesn't know anyone down there. She cries now when she thinks about it. Stay with her until spring . . . Until April . . . Kate is strong. She can take care of herself.

BEN   When did your mother ever have trouble making friends? In two weeks down there she'll be running for mayor . . . If she gets sick, if she needs me, I'll come to her . . . I have my own work to do. This country is getting richer every day from war profits. And whose pockets does it go into? To those who had the money before the war.

BLANCHE   Poppa, I'm not equipped to argue these things with you. I don't understand them. I never did. But I respect what you think is right. All I'm saying is, does it have to be in Brighton Beach? Can't you change the world from Florida?

BEN   You can change your bathing suits in Florida. Not the world.

BLANCHE   *(Crossing to the front door and looking out)*   Why do we have so much trouble understanding each other?

EUGENE   *(Entering* STAN's *room with the tray of sandwiches)*   Aunt Blanche is here. She's trying to get Grandpa to . . .

STAN   Shut up! Don't say anything! I'm thinking.

EUGENE   *(Sitting in the chair)*   Have you got an idea?

STAN   Will you shut up?

EUGENE   Tell me so I can think about it, too.

STAN   It's not an idea yet. It's the beginning of an idea. It's just a thought. A germ. A tiny speck in my mind. *(He inspects his sandwich)* You forgot the cucumbers.

EUGENE How about a college sketch? College sketches are always funny.

STAN *(Interested. Sitting on the ottoman)* Like what?

EUGENE Like this girl, Kathy O'Hara, from Mount Holyoke goes out on a blind date with a guy named Myron Isaac Eisenberg.

STAN I hate funny names. It's a cheap way of getting a laugh.

EUGENE I don't know. Why don't you try it out on Aunt Blanche?

BLANCHE What if, God forbid, Jack *did* leave her? What if the boys moved out? Saul and I can take care of her. She doesn't have to stay here. We could get a place in Florida for all three of you. Then you wouldn't have to worry, about Kate *or* Momma.
     (EUGENE leaves STAN's room and returns to his own)

BEN *(Rising and returning to his place at the dining table)* You think she would leave this house? You think she would take charity from her own sister?

BLANCHE *(Crossing above the sofa)* I took it from her when I needed it. Where was I going to go when Dave died? There's no shame in it when it's your own family. I would be paying her back for what she did for me and the girls.

BEN Don't you know your own sister better by now? . . . No. I don't think you do.

BLANCHE *(Crossing below the sofa)* Sometimes, Poppa, I think you don't approve of me . . . Sometimes, I think you don't even like me very much.

BEN   I have three daughters, and I love them the same. But the one who's in trouble is the one that I help.

BLANCHE   Doesn't that include your own wife? Why am I the only one in the family who wants to help Momma?

BEN   Because you're the only one who can afford it. Don't ask for too much, Blanche. When you live on Park Avenue, sympathy doesn't come with it.
   (BLANCHE *sits on the sofa*)

EUGENE (*Coming back into* STAN'*s room*)   What's new inside the old brain, Stan?

STAN   You're still an infant. I have a goddamn infant for a partner. Why don't you wait in your room. I'll call you when I think of it.

EUGENE   I want to help you.

STAN   I said, "Come back when I call you."

EUGENE (*At* STAN'*s door*)   Yes, Heathcliffe. I'll be waiting on the moors.
   (EUGENE *returns, again, to his own room and sits at the desk*)

STAN   And bring up the cucumbers!

EUGENE (*To audience*)   It's very hard writing with your brother, because your whole relationship gets in the way. Can you imagine *Hamlet* written by William and Harvey Shakespeare?
   (KATE *comes out of the kitchen with a hot plate of pot roast and vegetables, which she puts in front of* BEN. *She also has a small box wrapped in gift paper, which she gives to* BLANCHE)

KATE   This is for Nora's baby. If Nora doesn't like the color, I can exchange it.

BLANCHE I'm sure she'll love it. She's coming over Sunday with the baby. *(More to* BEN *than to* KATE*)* It would be a wonderful time for the whole family to get together. Before Momma leaves for Florida . . . Please come.

KATE It's a long trip on the train for Poppa.

BLANCHE I could send a car.

BEN A socialist sitting in the back of a Cadillac with a colored man driving?

BLANCHE You can let me know at the last minute . . .

KATE You sure you can't stay for dinner?

BLANCHE I told her we'd start to pack tonight. If I don't help her, she'd try to get her furniture in the suitcase . . . Poppa? Would you *call* Momma during the week and just say hello?

BEN I have a lot of meetings this week.

KATE He'll call.

BEN If I find the time.

KATE He'll call.

BLANCHE *(Crossing back to* KATE*)* I wish I could stay. I wish we had more time to talk. I'll call you tomorrow. *(She collects her things)* Sometimes I miss this house so much. I miss how good we were to each other.
    *(*BLANCHE *kisses* KATE *on the cheek)*

KATE Blanche! I need to talk to you. Not on the phone. Can we meet someplace in the city? Let me take you to lunch. Tomorrow, the next day. Whenever you can find time.

BLANCHE   Of course, Kate. Tomorrow. As early as you want.

KATE *(Tears welling in her eyes)*   I hate to ask you this. You know I never like to be obligated to anyone. But you're the only one I . . . *(Suddenly,* BEN, *who appeared to be nodding off at the table, drops his fork onto the plate. His breathing is heavy)* Poppa? What's wrong?
      (He is holding on to the table to balance himself)

BLANCHE *(Dropping her bag and package on the sofa)*   Oh my God!

KATE *(Taking* BEN's *hat off)*   What is it, Poppa? Is it a pain? Is it your chest?

BLANCHE *(Rushing to* BEN)   Oh, Poppa!

KATE   Try to breathe slowly. Deep breaths, Poppa.

BEN *(Sitting up straighter)*   It's all right. I'm all right.

KATE   You want some water? *(Pours him a glass of water)* Drink some water.

BLANCHE *(Taking* BEN's *hand)*   His hands are cold as ice.

KATE   Do you want to lie down?

BEN   I got dizzy for a second. *(Now fully recovered. To* KATE)   I was hungry. You could wait forever for something to eat around here.

BLANCHE   It's this climate. Two blocks from the ocean in February, how can you keep the cold out of the house?

BEN   It's not the cold. It's not the climate. It's nerves, that's what it is.

KATE   How do you know it's not your heart? You haven't seen a doctor in over a year.

BEN   A heart attack God gives you. Nerves you get from people who worry about you too much.

BLANCHE   Is that meant for me, Poppa?

KATE   It was meant for both of us. You learn not to pay attention. He doesn't mean it.

BLANCHE   He can't stand the winters here any more than Momma. *(She sits at the table)* I don't mean to upset you, Poppa. If you're happier here, then stay. Forget what we talked about. I'll get somebody to stay with Momma. I'll work it out myself.

KATE *(Returning* BEN's *hat to the closet)* All right, Blanche. Leave it alone for now. We've got time yet.

BLANCHE *(To* BEN*)*   Why is it so hard for us to talk to each other? Why is it so hard for you to take anything from me? I'm afraid to kiss you when I see you, I know how uncomfortable it makes you . . . Why is that, Poppa?

BEN *(Banging his fist on the table)* YOU ASK TOO MUCH OF ME! (KATE *and* BLANCHE *are stunned by this outburst)* I am not an affectionate man. I don't trust affection . . . Sometimes people give it to you instead of the truth.

BLANCHE *(Visibly hurt, going to sofa to collect her purse and package)*   I see . . . And what's the truth about me, Poppa? Have I betrayed you because the man I married became wealthy? When I met him, he was on the verge of bankruptcy. Whatever he got, he earned. Whatever he has, he worked for.

KATE Blanche, stop it. That's enough. Everybody has said enough.

BEN Let her say what she wants. She's a good girl, my Blanche, but sometimes she forgets where she came from . . . Is it cold outside, Blanche? You bet your life it is . . . Is it hard on the people who live out here? Ask them, they'll tell you . . . Take them *all* to Florida, they'll put up a statue of you on the boardwalk . . . But not even Saul could afford that. They all can't escape, Blanche. They all don't get a ticket to Miami.

BLANCHE And my sin is that I can afford to buy you one?

BEN There's no sin, Blanche. You're a generous woman. Even *I* can see that. I thank God you're able to take care of your mother. But I can't enjoy the benefits of a society that made my daughter rich and starves half the people in the country.

BLANCHE I can't take care of all the people in the country. I didn't ask for all this. I was happier when I had no money and Dave was alive. But I'm not going to curse God because He gave me a kind and loving husband and yes, a mink coat and a Cadillac car. You want them, take them. I didn't ask for it. I found the coat in my closet on my birthday. Some good it does me. It keeps out the cold, but it also stops my father from reaching out and holding me . . . Is that the politics you believe in, Poppa?

BEN I believe in what I was taught from the day I was born.

BLANCHE I believe in what I was taught, too . . . I was taught that a family who loves each other takes care of each other . . . You're seventy-seven years old, Poppa, you've done enough. You've worked hard all your life. It's time to play pinochle and walk on the beach. Maybe you'll meet a few retired socialists. *(Going to* KATE*)* I'll see you tomorrow, Kate?

KATE Let me see what happens. I'll call you in the morning.

BLANCHE *(Walks to the door, then turns to look at* BEN*)* I love you, Poppa . . . and I'll accept whatever affection you can give me. But you're not going to stop me and Momma from giving you ours. We're women, we don't know any better.
    *(*BLANCHE *exits)*

EUGENE *(From his bedroom, to audience)* Can you see now why I want to write comedy? Even God has a terrific sense of humor. Why else would He make Grandpa a dedicated socialist, fighting against the wealthy class, and then give him a daughter who marries the richest guy in the garment district? I wonder if we could sell it to CBS?
    *(*KATE *clears away* EUGENE*'s,* STAN*'s and her place settings. Then she turns out the porch light)*

KATE Why don't you finish your dinner?

BEN I'm not hungry anymore.

KATE You'll change your mind. I'll leave it in the oven.
    *(*KATE *takes* BEN*'s plate and starts toward the kitchen)*

BEN You think I don't know what's going on between you and Jack? That's what you wanted to talk to Blanche about, wasn't it?

KATE   You spoke to Jack?

BEN   I spoke to nobody. But you don't get to be seventy-seven without noticing a few things.

KATE   Nothing's going on.

BEN   If you can tell your sister, why can't you tell me?

KATE   I don't know. Maybe I'm afraid you'll think it's all my fault.

BEN   Is it?

KATE   You see? That's why I'm afraid to talk to you. (KATE *exits into the kitchen.* BEN *goes upstairs to his bedroom.* EUGENE *speaks from his bedroom to the audience)*

EUGENE   There's so much material in this house. Maybe I don't have to become a writer. If only I could get enough people to pay for seats in the living room.

STAN   (*Bursting into* EUGENE's *room, holding a sheet of paper)*   I can't believe it. I cannot believe it!

EUGENE   What?

STAN   I just came up with an idea. One of the funniest ideas I ever heard of in my life. I was hysterical just picturing it.

EUGENE   So what's wrong?

STAN   I just remembered I saw it on the Red Skelton show three weeks ago. (*He throws the paper into the wastebasket)* Can you imagine if we brought that in to CBS? They would grab us by our collars and crotches and throw us out in front of Abe Burrows.

EUGENE   Well, what was the idea? Maybe we could twist it around.

STAN Twist it around? We don't make pretzels, we write comedy. We're supposed to be original, think of *new* things. We don't steal from other people's shows.

EUGENE What are you, the district attorney of comedy?

STAN We're wasting time again. What have you got?

EUGENE *Me?* I don't have anything.

STAN Then what were you doing all this time?

EUGENE I was thinking of a way to grow cucumbers in my bedroom.

STAN God, you are lazy! Let me ask you something.

EUGENE Oh, God! I hate it when you say, "Let me ask you something."

STAN Let me ask you something. Are you serious about writing or not?

EUGENE Yes.

STAN Yes, what?

EUGENE Yes, I am serious about writing.

STAN No, I don't think you are.

EUGENE *(Jumping to his feet)* Oh, Jesus! . . . I am, Stanley. I am serious about writing. I'm kind of footloose and fancy-free about cucumbers, but I'm serious about writing.

STAN You can say what you want, I don't believe you are.

EUGENE I am! I am! *(To the heavens)* Please, Holy Mother, make my blind brother see that I speak the truth.

STAN All right. Tell me how serious you are about writing.

EUGENE Let me call a doctor, Stanley. I think you're cracking up.

STAN I want to know. I want to know just how serious you are about writing.

EUGENE *(Spreading his arms out wide, as though measuring a fish)* This much!

STAN Don't get sarcastic with me.

EUGENE That wasn't sarcastic. I was telling you point-blank I think you're crazy.

STAN You've been writing your memoirs since you're fourteen years old, and you still don't give a goddamn about your craft.

EUGENE It's not a craft, Stanley. A craft is Indian rug weaving. My memoirs is putting down the nutty things that have happened in my life. And this conversation is getting a whole chapter of its own.

STAN That's exactly what I mean. You may say you're serious about it, but you don't *act* serious.

EUGENE You want me to act serious about writing? . . . Okay. Watch! *(He strikes a very grim pose)* I would rather write a comedy sketch than feed all the starving children in the world.
    (He falls to the floor at STAN's *feet)*

STAN I could kill you right now. You want to forget about this? You want me to call CBS and tell them we're just not ready for this yet? Huh? Huh? All right?

EUGENE What are you getting so angry about?

STAN I'm not angry.

EUGENE Yes you are.

STAN I'm angry about your attitude.

EUGENE So why did you say you're not angry?

STAN Your attitude stinks, you know that?

EUGENE I can't believe this! Maybe to *you* my attitude stinks. To me, my attitude smells wonderful.

STAN *(Going to the door)* Listen, let's just forget about it. I don't think we can work together. I'm getting older, I don't have any more time to waste. I'll find somebody else.

EUGENE How about Abe Burrows? He's probably waiting for you on the elevator.

STAN No, that's what I'm going to do. I'm going to find somebody else. Someone with a bigger interest in his career than you have.

EUGENE *(Spreading out his arms again)* You mean bigger than this?

STAN You've got a lot to learn, my young friend.

EUGENE "My young friend"? . . . Jesus, now you're Abraham Lincoln! *(STAN storms out, into his own room. EUGENE follows)* You know what I think this is all about, Stanley? I think you're scared. I think it's a terrific way to put off sitting down and writing. That's what I think.
  (EUGENE returns to his own room)

STAN *(Following EUGENE)* Go on! Go visit your girl friend! I just hope to God she's got money and is willing to support you, because you'll never make a penny in this world on your own, you little shit!

(He slams EUGENE's *door, and goes back into his room)*

EUGENE *(To audience)*   See what I mean about brothers writing together!... They're too busy sibling all the time . . . But in a way, Stan was right. I wasn't concentrating because I was afraid I was losing the greatest girl in the world . . . Being in love is a definite career killer.

(The door opens and STAN *comes back in)*

STAN   I got another idea.

EUGENE *(To audience)*   But lucky for me, Stan was real dedicated. *(To* STAN*)* What's the idea?

STAN   Not an idea for a sketch. But I know what we've been doing wrong.

EUGENE   You do?

STAN   Tell me what you think we've been doing wrong.

EUGENE   What we've been doing wrong?

STAN *(Nods)*   What's the essential ingredient in every good sketch we've ever seen?

EUGENE   I don't know. What?

STAN   Don't say "what" so fast. Think about it.

EUGENE *(Thinks)*   What's the essential ingredient in every good sketch we've ever seen.

STAN   Right.

EUGENE   I don't know. What?

STAN   You *do* know. We've talked about it. You're just not thinking.

EUGENE Stan, I don't want to take a high school exam. Tell me so we can write the sketch.

STAN The ingredient in every good sketch we've ever seen—is conflict! . . . Remember? Remember the night we talked about conflict?

EUGENE Yes.

STAN You *do* remember?

EUGENE Tuesday, September seventh, eight thirty-five P.M.

STAN All right. Now what's the *other* ingredient in every good comedy sketch we've ever seen?

EUGENE *(Sighs in exasperation)* *More* conflict!

STAN Come on. You know it . . . Think about it . . . Heh? . . . Do you know it?

EUGENE Yes. It's when one brother wants to kill the other brother.

STAN YES!!

EUGENE Yes? That's it?

STAN It's close. You said it in that sentence. Do you remember what you said in that sentence?

EUGENE No. It was too long ago.

STAN One brother wants to kill the other brother. The key word is *wants!* In every comedy, even drama, somebody has to want something and want it bad. He wants money, he wants a girl, he wants to get to Philadelphia. When somebody tries to stop him from getting money or a girl or getting to Philadelphia, that's conflict. Wanting plus conflict equals what?

EUGENE *(Looking heavenward)* Oh please, God. Don't let me get it wrong. *(To* STAN*)* A job at CBS.

STAN Right.

EUGENE How do you know all this?

STAN I watch all the comedy shows. I make notes. I figure it out. I think scientifically. That's why I'm good at gin rummy. I always remember what the other guy picks up.

EUGENE So now that you know all this, do you have an idea for a sketch?

STAN No. Do you?

EUGENE Yeah. I think so.

STAN When did you think of it?

EUGENE While you were doing all that explaining to me.

STAN Well, tell it to me.

EUGENE Okay . . . there's a guy and a girl. They're in bed together.

STAN Who are they?

EUGENE No one. Just a guy and a girl.

STAN I know, but what do they do? Is he a cop? An insurance salesman? A doctor? What?

EUGENE It doesn't matter.

STAN Details are always better for a character. If he's a cop, maybe there's some police jokes in it.

EUGENE Okay. He's a cop. Patrolman John J. Mahoney. Fourth Precinct, Twenty-seventh District of

Manhattan on the night shift, ten to six. His partner is Patrolman Vito Manganezi, and he's married, with . . .

STAN All right, all right. You are some pain in the ass.

EUGENE So this cop is in bed with a girl . . . Maybe they're married.

STAN *Maybe* they're married?

EUGENE THEY'RE MARRIED! They had a wonderful wedding, four hundred guests, catered by the Paramount Caterers . . .

STAN I said all right! . . . Go on.
(*A loud knock on the bedroom door*)

BEN (*From outside the door*) Will you shut up in there! (STAN *opens the door*) (BEN *stands there in his pajamas*) I can't sleep! Go into another business!

EUGENE We're sorry, Grandpa. (*To* STAN) Come on. (EUGENE *and* STAN *run downstairs.* BEN *returns to his room*)

STAN Go on, go on . . . They're both in bed.

EUGENE They're both in bed. She has a broken leg.

STAN I like that.

EUGENE Thank God.
(*They sit on the sofa*)

STAN What time of year? . . . Winter, spring, summer?

EUGENE Winter. (STAN *stares at him*) Twenty-one degrees, winds fifteen miles per hour, barometer falling . . .

STAN Did I ask you? Go on.

EUGENE   It's two A.M. The window is open. It's freezing in the room. She asks him to get up to close the
window. He rushes over in his pajamas, but the
window is frozen. So he pushes down with all his
might—and slips his disk. He can't move. She can't
move. The window is still open, and they're both
freezing to death. How do they close the window?

STAN   How?

EUGENE   I don't know. It's only the beginning. I just
thought that two people who can't move in a freezing room with the window wide open was a funny
idea. Do you like it?

STAN   *(Pacing, thinking)*   I like some of it.

EUGENE   I only *told* you some of it. That's all there *is*
is some of it . . . What part didn't you like?

STAN   The logic. Why doesn't she call the doctor?

EUGENE *(Sitting in the armchair)*   I don't know . . . He's
not in. He went to a Broadway show.

STAN   At two in the morning?

EUGENE   They stole his car in the parking lot.

STAN   She could call another doctor.

EUGENE   They're at a convention in Cleveland.

STAN   Every single doctor in New York?

EUGENE   She broke her fingers. She can't dial.

STAN   All ten fingers?

EUGENE   It's just a comedy sketch. Does it have to be
so logical? We're not drawing the plans for the Suez
Canal.

45

STAN   Yes, we are. It's not funny if it's not believable.

EUGENE   Oh, you mean the Three Stooges are believable? Moe is fifty-five years old and wears bangs and sticks his fingers in his brothers' eyes.

STAN *(Crossing up to* EUGENE*)*   The Three Stooges? Is that the kind of comedy you want to write? That's for morons.

EUGENE   Really? Well, the morons made it to Hollywood, and the geniuses are freezing in Brighton Beach.

STAN   I'm not going to settle for crap. If we're going to be good, we're going to be the best.

EUGENE   Well, I can't think of anything else.

STAN *(Pacing)*   Let's keep trying.

EUGENE   Their phone is out of order?

STAN   Too easy. Too coincidental.

EUGENE   Too easy? It took me twenty minutes to think of it.

STAN *(Pacing around the sofa)*   Don't give up. Let me tell you the idea again. A guy and a girl are in bed together, okay? It's the middle of winter, and the window is open . . .

EUGENE   What if he's *not* a cop? What if he's a doctor? Then we don't have to worry about calling a doctor.

STAN   If he's a doctor, he fixes them both up. There's no sketch.

BEN *(Shouting from his bedroom)*   THAT'S FINE WITH ME!

46

STAN   So, she has a broken leg. He gets up. It's freezing in the room. He rushes over to close the window . . .

EUGENE   *(Leaping to his feet)*   . . . and he trips on the wire and pulls out the telephone cord.

STAN   . . . and they *can't* call the doctor! You know what we are, Gene? We're goddamn geniuses. *(He kisses* EUGENE *and they both run upstairs to* EUGENE'S *room)* Now we can begin! Now we can write the sketch! Come on!
      *(*STAN *leaps onto the bed, and* EUGENE *sits at his desk.* EUGENE *speaks to the audience)*

EUGENE   So at ten to seven in the evening, we had the idea for the sketch that would launch our careers, and we began to write. By eleven-thirty that night we had filled up three pads and had not written a single usable word.
      *(*KATE *comes out of the kitchen, and turns on the dining room lights. She sits at the table, waiting.*
      STAN *sits up and rubs his eyes)*

STAN   I can't keep my eyes open. You want to take a half-hour break?

EUGENE   How about an hour?

STAN   Thirty minutes. That's all. You have no discipline. Don't let me fall asleep.
      *(*STAN *exits to his own room, turns off the lights in both rooms. Both lie on their own beds.*
      JACK JEROME, *fifty-five years old and wearing an overcoat, rubbers, and hat, comes down the street and in the front door)*

JACK *(Surprised to see* KATE*)*   You still up?

KATE   I thought you might be hungry.

JACK *(Going to the closet to take off his coat and hat)*   I had dinner at work. They had food sent in. We have to get the spring line out by next Thursday. *(Sitting on the sofa to take off his rubbers)* Everybody's working overtime. Jacobsen is sleeping in his office.

KATE *(Collecting his rubbers and taking them to the closet)*   Oh, because you said you might be home tonight.

JACK   No, I told you. The whole week. Maybe into Monday or Tuesday. *(Standing and starting toward the stairs)* Everyone's exhausted. It's a wonder they're all not sick.

KATE   I have some tea heated up. Sit with me a few minutes.

JACK   Let me take a shower first. I'm all sweated up. I smell from the cutting room.

KATE   In thirty-three years, it's never bothered me before. I'll get the tea.
        (KATE exits into the kitchen. JACK takes off his suit coat and crosses to his seat at the head of the dining table)

JACK *(Calling into the kitchen)*   How are the boys?

KATE *(From the kitchen)*   I haven't seen them all night. They've been upstairs writing. Stanley thinks they might be able to get something in television.

JACK   Television? Ten people in this country have a television. There's no money unless there's volume. He's better off at Abraham and Straus.

KATE   If he gets this job, he wants to quit. Yesterday he looked for an apartment in the city. I think he and Eugene are getting ready to move out.

(KATE comes in from the kitchen with a tea service)

JACK He's going to pay New York rent on a job he doesn't have yet? He's got a good future at A & S, for God's sake. He's got security there. What do either one of them know about show business?

KATE *(Serving JACK his tea)* It's what they want to do.

JACK What you want to do and making a living are two different things. You don't keep a roof over your head doing what you *want* to do. You do what you *have* to do.

KATE I'm not saying you're wrong. But if they don't try this now, when will they ever have the chance?

JACK A chance at what? It's a one in a million shot. Who knows if they have talent? Did you ever see anything they wrote?

KATE They read me something once. They got upset because I didn't laugh. They didn't tell me it was supposed to be funny.

JACK If *you* didn't laugh, what chance do they have with the ten people with television sets? . . . It's crazy. It's not for them. I'll talk to Stanley tomorrow.

KATE *(Sitting down with her own tea)* It's not your decision, Jack. They're grown boys. They do what they want now . . . We don't need their money. It's only you, me, and Poppa now. And if Blanche can get Poppa to move to Florida, it'll just be the two of us. *(She pauses, looks at JACK)* It's a different world today. They have more opportunities than we did. You never had a chance to look around. You took the first job that came along . . . Sometimes I forget what you gave up to take care of a family.

JACK   Was I complaining? Did I say I gave up anything? I wasn't that brilliant or educated to give up
anything. But I made the most of what I did. Maybe
to some people I didn't accomplish anything important, but as a cutter, I'm one of the best. One of the
most respected, ask anybody.

KATE   I don't have to ask, Jack. I *know.*

JACK   You think I don't know what's on Stanley's
mind? You think I don't know what he's looking
for? . . . Actresses! Showgirls! That's what he's looking for. And for *that* he'll give up security and a
future.

KATE   Not everybody's looking for showgirls, Jack.

JACK   Is he afraid of hard work? Is he afraid of putting
in regular hours? I've done it for a lifetime, it hasn't
killed me.

KATE   No, Jack, it hasn't killed you. But the one thing
I was always sorry about was that you never did
something with your life that you enjoyed more.

JACK   I don't understand you. I've been a cutter for
thirty-three years, why do you bring up a thing like
that now for?

KATE   *(Stacking the empty cups and plates)*   Because you
seem different to me now. Because for the first time,
I see the unhappiness in your face. You look older
to me, Jack.

JACK   I look older because I'm older.

KATE   No. That's not what I see. What I see is disap-
pointment in your eyes.

JACK   *(Rising and crossing toward the stairs)*   I'll take a
shower and get a good night's sleep. It'll be gone in
the morning.

KATE I look every morning and it's never gone . . .
Maybe it's *me* you're disappointed with.

JACK *(Stopping at the sofa)* What are you talking about?

KATE *(Taking the tea service into the kitchen)* I don't
know what I'm talking about. You tell me, Jack.

JACK *(Calling after her, into the kitchen)* Tell you what?
You have something on your mind, then say it.

KATE *(Coming out of the kitchen, to the dining table)* If I
say what I'm thinking, you're liable to tell me what
I don't want to hear.

JACK Listen, Kate. I've had a long day. I'm tired.
Whatever this is about, we'll talk about it in the
morning.

KATE I want to know what you're planning to do.

JACK Planning to do about what?

KATE *(Folding the tablecloth carefully)* Whatever's been
going on, I want it to stop. I don't want to know
who she is or what she's like. And I don't want to
hear any lies. I just want tonight to be the end of it,
and I'll never talk about it again, as God is my judge.

JACK You think I'm carrying on with some woman?
Where do you get such ideas from?

KATE Two things a woman doesn't have to be told.
When she's pregnant and when her husband stops
loving her. Maybe we've had enough years of loving
each other. But I will not live out the rest of my life
being humiliated.

JACK Who's been talking to you? What goddamn liars
tell you such things? Nothing is going on. What's

happened to us when we can't believe each other anymore?

KATE Maybe it's the way you look at me when you say you're telling me the truth.

JACK *(Deliberately)* There is no other woman.

KATE Why not?

JACK What?

KATE Why not? You're a healthy man, you're affectionate, you're as normal as anyone else. We haven't been together as man and wife since God knows when. So, if it's not me and you're swearing it's no one else, I'm asking you, Why not?

JACK Kate, let's not get into this. I beg of you.

KATE *Don't beg me!!* . . . Don't tell me how trusting we were. We passed all that when our children grew up. Now it's just you and me, Jack, and if I'm not enough for you anymore, then you tell me and get out. Get out, goddamn it! I will not be pointed at from windows as I walk down the street.

JACK There is no other woman.

KATE I don't care. Stop it anyway.

JACK Look, I know I've changed. I know I'm different.

KATE Yes, you are.

JACK I've stopped feeling for everything. Getting up in the morning, going to bed at night . . . Why do I do it? Maybe it was the war. The war came along and after that, nothing was the same. I hated poverty, but I knew how to deal with it. I don't know

my place anymore. When I was a boy in temple, I looked at the old men and thought, "They're so wise. They must know all the secrets of the world" ... I'm a middle-aged man and I don't know a damn thing. Wisdom doesn't come with age. It comes with wisdom ... I'm not wise, and I never will be ... I don't even lie very well ... There was a woman. (KATE *stares at him*) About a year ago. I met her in a restaurant on Seventh Avenue. She worked in a bank, a widow. Not all that attractive, but a refined woman, spoke very well, better educated than I was ... It was a year ago, Kate. It didn't last long. I never thought it would ... and it's over now. If I've hurt you, and God knows you have every right to be, then I apologize. I'm sorry. But I'll be truthful with you. I didn't tell it to you just now out of a great sense of honesty. I told you because I couldn't carry the weight of all that guilt on my back anymore.
(JACK *waits quietly for her reaction*)

KATE How old a woman?

JACK Don't get into that, Kate. If you want to have your anger, throw something at me. But don't ask me questions about her. Let's talk about you and me. Tell me how we can get through this thing, but who and what she is is not important anymore.

KATE How old a woman?

JACK God Almighty, you won't be happy until you dig into it, will you? ... Forty-four, forty-five, I don't know. I never asked her.

KATE What did you talk about?

JACK When?

KATE   That first day in the restaurant.

JACK   I don't remember. We just talked.

KATE   It must have been about something. The soup? The chicken? The fruit cup? How do these things start, Jack? I never heard one before.

JACK   I don't know who you're trying to hurt more, Kate. You or me.

KATE   What did you say in the restaurant, Jack?

JACK   Anything. Everything. We talked about the weather, about politics, about music, our children...

KATE   You get forty-five minutes for lunch. Besides eating, that's a lot of ground to cover, wasn't it?

JACK   Yes, it was a lot of ground to cover. Is that the answer you want, Kate?

KATE   Why her? After thirty-three years of marriage, why is she the one you picked?

JACK   Don't! For crise-sakes, don't make me say nice things about her. You want me to say she was a tramp? Okay, she was a tramp. I had an affair with a peroxide-blond tramp, Kate. Is that all right?

KATE   I wish to God you did. A tramp I could handle. But that's not your nature, Jack ... And I want to know why *this* woman was the one.

JACK   This is a mistake, Kate. A mistake we'll both regret, as God is my judge ... Why this woman? Because she had an interest in life besides working in a bank or taking care of her house. To her, the world was bigger than that. She read books I never heard of, talked about places I never knew existed. When she talked, I just listened. And when *I* talked, I suddenly heard myself say things I never knew I felt. Because she asked questions that I had to answer . . . Learning about yourself can be a very dangerous thing, Kate. Some people, like me, should leave well enough alone . . . The things you were afraid to hear, I won't tell you, because they're true. It lasted less time than you think, but once was enough to hurt, I realize that . . . I never ate in that restaurant again, and I have never once seen her again . . . If either one of us feels better now that I've told you all that, then shame on both of us. (JACK *sits at the table, opposite* KATE. *She turns away from him*) If I killed a man on the street, you would probably stand by me. Maybe even understand it. So why is this the greatest sin that can happen to a man and wife?

KATE Because I'm not strong enough to forgive it.

JACK I didn't expect you to.

KATE What *do* you expect?

JACK I'm not clever enough to answer that.

KATE This woman—this refined, educated woman— if I left you, would you go to her?

JACK She wouldn't have me. She's content with her life the way it is.

KATE If she *would* have you, would you go to her?

JACK No.

KATE Why not?

JACK Because I know where I belong.

KATE   Here? Is this where you belong, Jack? In a house with a woman who hasn't read the right books or traveled any further in the world than the subway could take her? I take care of a house and I raised a family, but I don't know the questions to ask you that will make you feel things you never felt before. No, I don't think this is where you belong anymore, Jack.

JACK   If I felt that, I would have left last year.

KATE *(Rising)*   You did leave, Jack. You never moved out, but you left.

JACK   I know we've not been the same together. Not for a long time. And for that, I'm sorry.

KATE   So you stay with me because she won't have you . . . I got some bargain, didn't I, Jack?

JACK   . . . So? What do you want to do?

KATE   What do *I* want to do? Is that how it works? You have an affair, and I get the choice of forgetting about it or living alone for the rest of my life? . . . It's so simple for you, isn't it? I am so angry. I am so hurt by your selfishness. You break what was good between us and leave me to pick up the pieces . . . and *still* you continue to lie to me.

JACK   I told you everything.

KATE *(Sitting in the upstage dining chair)*   I knew about that woman a year ago. I got a phone call from a friend, I won't even tell you who . . . "What's going on with you and Jack?" she asks me. "Are you two still together? Who's this woman he's having lunch with every day?" she asks me. . . . I said, "Did you see them together?" . . . She said, "No, but I heard."

. . . I said, "Don't believe what you hear. Believe what you see!" and I hung up on her . . . Did I do good, Jack? Did I defend my husband like a good wife? . . . A year I lived with that, hoping to God it wasn't true and, if it was, praying it would go away . . . And God was good to me. No more phone calls, no more stories about Jack and his lunch partner . . . No more wondering why you were coming home late from work even when it wasn't the busy season . . . Until this morning. Guess who calls me? . . . Guess who Jack was having lunch with in the same restaurant twice last week? . . . Last year's lies don't hold up this year, Jack . . . This year you have to deal with it.

(JACK *looks at her, remains silent a moment*)

JACK . . . It's true. I saw her last week. Twice in the same restaurant, once in another restaurant.

KATE And where else, Jack? Do you always sit or do you lie down once in a while? *(Rising)* Twice tonight I went to the phone to see if you were really working, but I was so afraid to hear that you left early, I couldn't dial the number . . . How is it possible I could hate you so much after loving you all my life?

JACK Would you believe me if I told you it was lunch and nothing else?

KATE *(Crossing to the stairs)* I can't talk about this anymore . . . Sleep down here. Anywhere you want except next to me.

JACK She's just a friend now, Kate. That's all.

KATE Is that what you tell her I am? Just a wife? *(She starts up the stairs)*

JACK   She left her job for six months. I knew what had happened, but I couldn't get in touch with her. Her son was killed in an automobile accident . . . So I have lunch with her and talk about anything else except the accident.

KATE *(Coming back down to the foot of the stairs)*   If you see her again, you take your things and move out of this house.
        (She starts back up the stairs)

JACK   I slept with her before and you forgave me. Now I buy the woman lunch and offer her compassion and for this you want to end the marriage.

KATE *(Coming back downstairs, close to* JACK*)*   I didn't expect to get through a lifetime without you touching another woman. But having feelings for her is something I can never forgive.
        *(*KATE *goes upstairs into her bedroom.* JACK *sits at the table for a moment, then goes into the kitchen.*
        A subway train is heard in the distance.
        STAN *suddenly sits up in bed. He turns on his light and looks at his watch. He rushes into* EUGENE*'s room and turns on* EUGENE*'s light. He shakes* EUGENE*)*

STAN   Why didn't you wake me?

EUGENE *(Struggling out of a sound sleep)*   What?

STAN   I told you to wake me at twelve-thirty.

EUGENE   What time is it?

STAN   Twenty-five to one. We overslept.

EUGENE   Five minutes! You're yelling about five minutes?

STAN *(Hopping around the room, slapping his face)*   Come on! Get up! If we fall asleep again, we're dead. Get your blood going. Move! Get oxygen into your brains.

EUGENE *(Sitting up)*   Don't slap me. My brains are up.

STAN   Read back what we have.

EUGENE   The whole thing?

STAN   From the beginning.

EUGENE *(Flipping through the pads)*   We don't have any-thing.

STAN   Read the stuff we crossed out.

EUGENE   It's all crossed out.

STAN   Read it anyway. If I hear it again, then I'll know why it was wrong. Then we can get it right.

EUGENE   There's three pads of it. We'll spend an hour reading back what took us four hours to write what we didn't like.

STAN   Stop fighting me all the time. The more you fight me, the more pressure I feel. I need my head clear, I don't need it full of pressure. Just read it, will you, please!

EUGENE *(Reading from the first pad)*   "A bedroom, about midnight. It is February and we see frost on the windows. One of the windows is open and we see the curtain blowing in. We hear teeth chattering from the bed . . ."

STAN   I can't hear it! I can't concentrate! I can't focus on anything! . . . Can you hear it?

EUGENE   Yeah, but I'm sitting a lot closer to me.

STAN   Let me talk to myself for a minute. *(He walks to a corner of the room)* Stop it, Stanley! Stop and listen to what he's reading. You've waited your whole life for this, don't be a schmuck. *(He takes a deep breath and turns back to* EUGENE*)* Okay. Read the rest.

EUGENE *(Reading from the first pad)* "A woman speaks. Her name is Shirley. Shirley says—" *(He squints at the page)* I can't read it. The rest is crossed out.

STAN *(Taking the pad from* EUGENE*)* Let me see it. *(He looks at the pad)* What did you black it out for? When you cross something out, you just put a line through it. *(Pointing a finger at* EUGENE*) Never* black out anything anymore, do you hear me? I want a thin, simple line.

EUGENE You want me to take a drawing class?

STAN Let's get another idea. If we're stuck this long, there must be something wrong with it.

EUGENE It's going to take just as long to get another idea.

STAN My head is tightening up. I'm all constricted inside. I just can't think. *(He thinks, then looks at* EUGENE*)* This is hard, Gene. Really hard.

EUGENE I know.

STAN I won't give up if you don't give up.

EUGENE I won't give up.

STAN I love being a writer.

EUGENE Me, too.

STAN It's just the writing that's hard . . . You know what I mean?

EUGENE Yeah.

STAN   Maybe I could be a rewriter . . . I'm terrific at fixing up things that are already written.

EUGENE   Like an editor. Every writer needs an editor.

STAN   . . . I don't want to hold you back, Gene. If we don't come up with this sketch, if we don't get this job, I don't want it to stop you.

EUGENE   We'll come up with it. You just have to relax.

STAN   Because there are two writers I know. Marvin Rose and Alan Zweicker. They wrote something for Milton Berle once. They would take you on if I asked them.

EUGENE   Don't ask them. I don't want to write with someone else.

STAN   No, they're really good. Not as good as us, but you could at least make a living with them.

EUGENE   If they're not as good as us, what are we stopping for?

STAN   We're not stopping. I'm just planning ahead. Like I do in gin rummy . . . We could be the greatest, Gene. The greatest comedy writers in America . . . I just have to learn to deal with the pressure.

EUGENE   So do I. It's not easy for me either.

STAN   I'm feeling better. I'm glad we had this talk. It reassures me that you want to stick with me. I'm feeling more relaxed now.

EUGENE   So am I.

STAN   . . . Now if we can just get an idea.

EUGENE   We will. I know we will.

STAN *(Looking up)*   Oh, God. Give us an idea, God! I'm here, God. Tell it to me. Give us an idea for a sketch you're not using. Tell me an idea that makes you laugh.

(EUGENE *looks up to see if God is going to do it)*
Curtain

One month later.

A few minutes before 6:00 P.M. on a Saturday night. It is dark outside and snow is even higher than before. It's a rough winter.

EUGENE *is sitting up in bed in pajamas, robe, slippers, and white sweat socks. His desk chair serves as a night table and on it are medicine and orange juice. He wipes his nose with an old handkerchief.*

EUGENE *(To audience)* It was the biggest night of my life and here I was, sick in bed. I took Josie ice skating at Rockefeller Center and fell down seven times and came home with a hundred and two temperature. Jewish guys are never good at sports played between November and April.

> *(STAN leaves his bedroom and comes downstairs. He looks out the front window toward the subway, then sets about rearranging the furniture, the better to hear the radio. KATE enters from the kitchen and puts some festive doilies on the dining table)*

... We came in with a finished sketch a few days late, and although CBS didn't think we were ready for big-time television, they did put us on small-time radio. Saturday night at six o'clock, when everyone's getting dressed or eating dinner, but not listening to CBS radio. It was an experimental comedy show to develop new talent and there were six young writers. We knew our future was on the line that night, but it wasn't CBS we were worried about. It was Mom and Pop's approval that meant the most to us.

> *(STAN brings a dining chair next to the sofa as KATE enters from the kitchen with a bowl of fruit and a bowl of nuts)*

STAN No, MA!! No fruit! No nuts! No food at all.

KATE Why not?

STAN You want a room full of people eating cashew nuts? They won't hear *any*thing!

KATE They could eat fruit. Bananas and oranges don't make noise.
(*She puts the fruit on the table*)

STAN (*Looks at his watch, then dashes to the front door*) Nine minutes to six and Pop's not home. I don't believe it. Of all nights in the world.

KATE (*Going to the foot of the stairs*) I don't know what to do about Eugene. He shouldn't be coming downstairs with the flu.

STAN He'd be down here with leprosy. We'd pile up the pieces in a chair next to the radio. You think he's going to miss this? (KATE *goes to the breakfront and takes out candlesticks, which she puts on the table*) Where's Grandpa? Did you call him?

KATE He's taking his nap. I'll wake him just before it goes on.

STAN We've got nine minutes!! It takes him twelve minutes to get his slippers on. (*Calling up the stairs*) GRANDPA!! . . . Come on down! The show is on!!

KATE (*Returning the dining chair to its proper spot*) What kind of cookies do you want with the tea?

STAN NO TEA! NO COOKIES!! . . . That's all I need is rattling cups and you saying, "Watch your crumbs."

KATE (*Entering the kitchen*) I was doing it for you, not for me.

STAN Then don't do it for me. I want it to be quiet
so you can hear the laughs. *(He turns on the radio)*
What's the matter with the radio? Is it plugged in?
(He looks behind the radio. KATE *brings a tray of teacups
from the kitchen to the breakfront)* The radio is broken.
I can't believe THE RADIO IS BROKEN!!

KATE You have to let it warm up first.

STAN It never takes this long. NO, NO, NO!! IT'S
BROKEN!!
  *(He throws himself on the floor. The radio comes on.
  We hear dance music)*

KATE You see!

STAN *(Going to the radio to fine-tune it)* Is that clear?
That doesn't sound clear to me. Can you hear it?

KATE I hear it fine.

STAN It's all the ice on the wires. I hate the winter.

KATE *(Coming to* STAN *at the radio)* You're going to get
an ulcer, Stanley. You were never this nervous at
Abraham and Straus.

STAN Because no one tuned in to listen to me selling
boys' clothing. *(He turns off the radio, then crosses to the
front door and looks out)* I don't see Pop. I don't even
hear the train.

KATE *(Joining* STAN *at the front door)* You told him six
o'clock?

STAN Five hundred times. I pinned it on his pajamas
last night. Where could he be?

KATE I don't know. I'll go wake up Grandpa.

STAN I'll do it. You turn off the tea. It'll start to whistle in the middle of the program.

(KATE goes into the kitchen. STAN opens the front door and steps out into the cold, looking for his father. Then he comes back in and starts up the stairs)

EUGENE *(Sneezes. Then, to audience)* Mom and Pop were still together, but you'd never notice it. Almost a month had gone by since the big fight, and they barely spoke to each other. And when they did speak, they spoke in the third person. "Is he coming home for dinner tonight?" "He's not sure. He'll let her know." "She doesn't care. Let him do what he wants." I kept looking around to see if there was another couple there.

STAN *(Opening EUGENE's bedroom door)* Let's go. We're on the air. *(Knocking on BEN's door)* Grandpa! Come on. This is it! Gene and I are going to become capitalists! *(To EUGENE, as they come downstairs)* Pop's not home yet.

EUGENE You're kidding.

STAN *(Coming into the living room and again putting the dining chair next to the sofa)* This is some audience we've got. A mother who doesn't talk to a father who hasn't come home yet, and a grandfather who hasn't laughed since the stock market crashed.

EUGENE *(Coming slowly down the stairs)* My hair hurts. My pajamas hurt.

KATE *(Going to the foot of the stairs and holding up her hand for EUGENE to put his forehead on)* You have a hundred and two fever.
 (She returns the dining chair to its proper place)

EUGENE Why did they waste years developing the thermometer? You could make a fortune just feeling people in hospitals.

(BEN comes down the stairs. EUGENE sits in the arm-chair. In the distance we hear the subway, and STAN comes running out of the kitchen to the front door)

STAN   There's the train. *(Looks at his watch)* Even if he runs, he'll never make it on time.

BEN *(At the foot of the stairs)*   Have I got time to go to the bathroom?

STAN   We're on in three minutes.

KATE *(To BEN)*   You go when you have to go. Go on.

BEN   You got today's paper?

STAN   The *paper?* We won't see you till Tuesday! *(More reasonably)* Didn't I hear you in the bathroom five minutes ago, Gramps?

BEN   Was that me? You're right. Forget it. I don't have to go.

STAN *(Seeing EUGENE in the armchair)*   Not there. That's Pop's chair. Sit over there.

KATE *(Seeing EUGENE about to sit on the sofa)*   Not there. There's always a draft in that spot.

BEN *(Seeing EUGENE about to sit on the other end of the sofa)*   Let me sit there. I have to put my feet up. They're swollen again.

EUGENE *(Standing in the middle of the living room)*   Boy, this is the toughest seat in town to get.
    (KATE pushes a dining chair next to the sofa for EU-GENE, then puts some pillows under BEN's head)

STAN *(Looking out the front windows)*   There's a few people getting off. It's so dark. I can't make out anyone.

BEN *(Stretching out on the sofa. To EUGENE)*   So, what kind of a story is this?

69

EUGENE   It's not a story. It's a variety show. It's music and sketches and monologues and comedy inter-views. It's entertainment.

BEN   Why, because they have nothing to say?

EUGENE   It's not *supposed* to say anything.

BEN   There's nothing to say? With three quarters of the world in economic slavery, there's nothing to say?

STAN *(Sitting in the armchair)*   They didn't want any sketches on economic slavery, Grandpa. They're looking for laughs, not an uprising.

KATE *(Taking her knitting from the breakfront)*   There's nothing wrong with a good laugh. We could all use a good laugh these days.

EUGENE   What time is it?

STAN *(Looking at his watch)*   Jesus! It's almost on. And he's not home yet.
     (He goes to the front door and looks out)

EUGENE   God, my heart is pounding.

KATE *(Taking dates from the breakfront)*   Does anyone want some dates? Dates don't make noise.
     (She gives a date to BEN, then sits in the armchair)

STAN   NO, MA! Nobody wants anything.

EUGENE   Please, God, don't let us be humiliated.

KATE   Aunt Blanche has all her friends listening. Grandma has everybody in her apartment in Miami . . . Everybody in Brighton Beach is tuned in.

BEN   But try to get them to read a newspaper, they're too busy.

STAN *(At the radio, adjusting the volume. The "Chubby Waters Show" theme music comes on)* Shhh! Here it comes! This is it!

EUGENE Good luck, Stan.

STAN *(Going to* EUGENE, *shaking his hand, then coming back to sit in front of the radio)* Good luck, Eug!
(From the radio, after the theme music, we hear the announcer)

ANNOUNCER From New York City, the Columbia Broadcasting System presents "The Chubby Waters Show," starring Chubby Waters and featuring Fred C. Sherman, Grace Dooley, Don Paloma, Sarah MacLaren, John Dunninger, Dick Ambrose and his Waldorf-Astoria Orchestra, and special guest star Pepito, the only Spanish-speaking dog in the English-speaking world.
(The theme music continues under the following)

BEN *(To* EUGENE) They have a Spanish-speaking dog?

EUGENE Wait'll you hear him. He's hysterical.

BEN He really speaks Spanish, or they taught it to him?

STAN He can bark, "Si, si." Whatever you ask him, he says, "Si, si."

BEN *(To* STAN *and* KATE) If he speaks Spanish, the audience won't understand. They're not as smart as the dog.

KATE Why didn't they say your names?

EUGENE At the end of the program . . . if they have time. Shh. It's on again.

ANNOUNCER *(From the radio)* And now, the star of "The Chubby Waters Show," Mr. Chubby Waters. *(The studio audience applauds)*

KATE *(To* STAN, *whose head is pressed to the radio grill-work)* Get your head away from there, Stanley. You'll go deaf.

CHUBBY *(From the radio)* Thank you. Thank you, ladies and gentlemen . . . I'm kinda nervous, this being my first big-time New York program. I'm from Decatur, Illinois, and our humor is a lot slower out there . . . I had my own program in Decatur and when I told a joke, they didn't laugh until next week's show. *(The studio audience laughs)*

BEN Oi vay!

CHUBBY Decatur's kind of a small town. I'll tell you how small it is. Some guys drove through town and threw a snowball at us . . . and we were shoveling it out for a week. *(The studio audience laughs)*

KATE Did that really happen?

EUGENE No, Ma. It's just a joke.

STAN Shhhh, will you please.

CHUBBY Decatur's sort of an agricultural town. We sell all the fruit and vegetables that drop offa trucks passing through. *(The studio audience laughs)*

BEN Only in America this man makes a living.

STAN *(To* BEN*)* Are you going to do this all night?

CHUBBY The census taker told us the average family in Decatur has about two and a half children. Most families prefer to have two girls and half a boy. *(The studio audience laughs)* The reason being that with half a girl, you still got to buy the whole dress, but with half a boy, you only got to buy the pants.
(The studio audience laughs and applauds)

BEN *(To EUGENE)* You wrote that?

EUGENE No. One of the other guys.

BEN Stay away from him. He's crazy.

STAN Great. Can't even hear the program in my own house.

CHUBBY When Abe Lincoln left Springfield, Illinois, his first speech was supposed to be Decatur. But his legs were too long, and darned if he didn't step over us.
(The studio audience laughs)

BEN In Russia, he'd be shot by now.

STAN I can't believe this. My own grandfather.

CHUBBY The folks back home are really rootin' for me. Because if I don't make good, I'll have to go back to Decatur, but a new baby was born there yesterday, and, well, I lost my space.
(The studio audience laughs)

KATE Why is he telling us all this?
(STAN gets up and walks to the dining room to calm himself)

EUGENE It's a monologue. He's warming up the audience.

BEN   They'd be better off sending up heat.

CHUBBY   'Preciate meetin' ya. I'll be right back, when I make my first tour through New York City and meet the Pitkin family of Coney Island, Brooklyn, New York.

STAN   That's ours! Ours is next. (*Dick Ambrose and his orchestra plays over the radio. The front door opens, and* JACK *rushes in*) Pop! You just made it! You're just in time! Our sketch is next.
> (KATE *gets up from the armchair and goes to the dining table and her knitting.* STAN *helps* JACK *off with his coat*)

JACK   I'm sorry I'm late. I couldn't help it.

EUGENE   It's okay. You didn't miss anything. You timed it on the button.

STAN   Sit in the armchair, Pop. You can hear perfectly.

JACK   Three trains were frozen to the tracks. It's some mess out there.

STAN   (*Ushering* JACK *to the armchair, and then sitting in front of the radio*)   Sit down, Pop... The comedian's name is Chubby Waters... He's a little corny, but the network likes that.

EUGENE   He's about to visit the Pitkin family from Coney Island. That's ours.

KATE   Does he want anything to eat?

JACK   He'll take something after... Thank her anyway.

EUGENE   (*To audience*)   You're not going to get big laughs from people who call each other "him" and "her!"

(Dick Ambrose and his orchestra finish. The studio audience applauds)

ANNOUNCER *(From the radio)* . . . Newly arrived in New York, Mr. Charles "Chubby" Waters decides to visit the city he's always dreamed of, ever since he was born half a child in Decatur, Illinois.

STAN *(To JACK)* I'll explain that later, Pop.

ANNOUNCER But it's not the Empire State or the Statue of Liberty or Grant's Tomb that Mr. Waters wants to see. It's the people; for it's the people who make our cities great. And so he decided to take the subway. Being half a person, he walks under the turnstile and rides out to Coney Island. He gets off, smelling the fresh sea water and the stale frankfurter rolls, and walks through the historic streets . . . and rings the bell of Mr. and Mrs. Morris Pitkin.
(We hear a doorbell ring)

EUGENE *(To BEN)* That's sound effects.
(We hear a door open)

MRS. PITKIN *(From the radio)* Yes?

CHUBBY *(From the radio)* How do you do? My name is Chubby Waters. May I ask, have you ever heard of me?

MRS. PITKIN Not that I heard of.
(A small laugh from the studio audience)

CHUBBY Well, I'm a radio comedian, and I have a brand new show on CBS starting this Saturday night at six. Will you be listening to it?

MRS. PITKIN Only if *you* can make a pot roast.
(A bigger laugh from the studio audience)

75

CHUBBY   Is that anything like a roast ham?

MRS. PITKIN   Not in this neighborhood.
(*A big studio laugh*)

CHUBBY   I'm trying to familiarize myself with New Yorkers, and I wondered if I could come in and say hello to your family.

MRS. PITKIN   Why? My *family* doesn't say hello to my family.
(*Studio laugh*)

CHUBBY   I don't mean to impose, but it would be very helpful to me. I'd be most grateful.

MRS. PITKIN   All right . . . Wipe your feet.

CHUBBY   Certainly. (*Sound effect of wiping feet*) . . . There! They're clean.

MRS. PITKIN   Your *shoes* are clean. I meant the *feet*. Take your socks off too.
(*Studio laugh*)

CHUBBY   Certainly . . . There! Now everything's clean . . . Oh, what a pretty house. I like your furniture. What style would you call it?

MRS. PITKIN   Sacrifice! That's what you have to do to get it.
(*Studio laugh*)

KATE   She reminds me of someone, but I can't think who.

CHUBBY   Is that a new rug?

MRS. PITKIN   Where?

CHUBBY   That thing rolled up in the corner.

MRS. PITKIN No. That's my father-in-law.
  (Studio laugh)

CHUBBY He sleeps on the floor?

MRS. PITKIN He likes to sleep on newspapers, because if he wakes up in the middle of the night, he's got something to read.
  (Studio laugh)

CHUBBY A well-read bed . . .

MRS. PITKIN Step over the papers, please. If you get print on your bare feet, it'll be all over my father-in-law.
  (Studio laugh)

CHUBBY I'll put my socks back on . . . Is it possible to meet your husband?

MRS. PITKIN Sure. Do what I do. Write in for an appointment. *(Studio laugh)* He's in here. But be quiet. He's working.

CHUBBY What does he do?

MRS. PITKIN He's in ladies' pajamas.
  (Studio laugh)

CHUBBY How do you feel about your husband being in ladies' pajamas?

MRS. PITKIN That's the sacrifice I had to make to get the furniture.
  (Big studio laugh and applause. The sound of the radio show becomes muted, almost inaudible, they all listen, except EUGENE, who turns to the audience)

EUGENE . . . Practically everything we wrote scored a bull's-eye . . . The only sad note was that although

77

we were a smash at CBS, we came up real short in the living room in Brighton Beach . . . The thirty minutes went by about as quickly as the Middle Ages . . . Finally, our agony was over.
> *(The sound of the radio show comes up again. The theme music is playing at a fast tempo and we hear the* ANNOUNCER *rattling off the credits)*

ANNOUNCER "The Chubby Waters Show" was a Steve Coleman-Mel Jason Production in association with the Columbia Broadcasting System . . . Pepito the talking dog appeared through the courtesy of R.K.O. Pictures . . . The producer of "The Chubby Waters Show" is Jeff Bishop, directed by Todd Allen and written by Michael Solomon, Larry Shapiro, Frank Connally, Donald Kreiss, and Stanley and Eugene Gerard.

STAN *(As he and* EUGENE *look dumbfounded at the radio)* *JEROME!!!*

ANNOUNCER Good night from New York to all of you from all of us.
> *(*STANLEY *switches off the radio)*

STAN *(Shouting at the radio)* You couldn't even remember Jerome, you stupid idiot! *(Storming into the dining room)* Gerard doesn't even sound like Jerome. I'm calling a lawyer. I should have been at rehearsals.

EUGENE It was a great audience, though, wasn't it?

STAN We got through it, Eug. At least, we got through it.
> *(The boys stare at* KATE*)*

KATE Well, I liked it. It was lively. The actors were good. Everybody remembered their lines.

STAN It's radio, Ma. They read them from scripts.

EUGENE (*Returning his dining chair to the table*) But did you really, really like it, Ma?

KATE What do you mean, did I like it? Didn't you hear the audience laughing?

EUGENE That was them, not you.

KATE (*Going to the closet for her coat*) There were too many funny lines. They came so fast, I couldn't find a place to laugh. Next week make it slower.

STAN Where are you going?

KATE I have to go next door to Mrs. Slutsky's to borrow some honey for this one's tea. (*Kissing* EUGENE) I'm very proud of both of you.
    (*She kisses* STAN)

STAN I can go.

KATE You have a date in half an hour, don't you? It's worth it for me to catch a cold to see you get married.
    (*She exits through the back door. The boys turn their gaze on* BEN)

BEN (*Rising slowly*) I'm going to finish my nap.

STAN You didn't like it. I can tell.

BEN (*Crossing toward the stairs*) I didn't hate it either. When I don't hate something, it's not bad.

EUGENE What was wrong with it?

BEN To me, comedy has to have a point. What was the point of this?

EUGENE To make people laugh.

BEN That's not a point. To make people *aware,* that's a point. Political satire, that's what you should have written. You could change half the world with political satire. Think about that sometime.

EUGENE Political satire? We're lucky we came up with a few good jokes.

BEN *(On the stairs)* I'll teach you how to write it. You sneak in a few remarks about what's wrong with this political system. If you make it funny enough, CBS will never notice.

EUGENE *(To* STAN*)* Can't you just see it? . . . "The Socialist Revue" starring Chubby Trotsky . . . We'd be writing it from jail.

BEN I liked the talking dog. "Si, si!" He didn't make any points, but he made me laugh. "Si, si!"
*(*BEN *continues up the stairs and to his bedroom)*

STAN You haven't said anything yet, Pop. Is anything wrong?

JACK I tell you the truth, I had a hard time listening.

EUGENE Why?

JACK Sit down. Both of you. *(They sit on the sofa)* That was us you were writing about tonight, wasn't it? The family.

STAN No. Not really.

JACK Not really? You don't think you made fun of this family tonight?

STAN *(After a look to* EUGENE*)* No. We weren't thinking of the family. It's all the people we know. Here in Brighton Beach or Coney Island or Brooklyn. People we grew up with. It's no one particular.

JACK I'm willing to give you the benefit of the doubt. But listen: The woman says to the man, "My family doesn't say hello to my family." That wasn't your mother? If that wasn't your mother, who was it?

EUGENE It's every mother who lives out here. They all talk like that. That's what happens in neighborhoods. Everyone sounds alike.

JACK Everyone in this area knows about your grandfather. He falls asleep on buses, on trains, in the library. So you have a grandfather on the show who falls asleep on newspapers on the floor. The people out here who are listening know who you're talking about. And you're not ashamed to put a thing like that on the radio?

STAN He heard it. He didn't say a word. He never thought it was him.

JACK I don't care if he said a word or not. *I* knew it was him and *you* knew it was him. It makes no difference who he thought it was. You don't poke fun of your own grandfather in front of the whole world.
    (He takes his rubbers to the closet)

EUGENE We'd never poke fun at him. We love Grandpa. But old people fall asleep a lot, so we just wrote it down. It's just a coincidence.

JACK *(Pacing angrily)* And what about her husband? What did you say about him on the radio?

STAN Nothing.

JACK Nothing? . . . Eugene, on the program, what does the woman say her husband does for a living?

EUGENE He's in ladies' pajamas.

JACK   And I'm in ladies' raincoats, right?

EUGENE   A man being in ladies' pajamas just sounds funny. It's a joke.

JACK   Are you going to pretend you don't know what's going on between your mother and me? ... Heh? ... You're not deaf, you're not blind, so you must know something, right? *(The boys say nothing)* I don't know what she tells you. I don't know what stories she fills your head with. God knows what she must say to you about me.

STAN   She never said anything to me, I swear.

JACK   But you know what's going on, don't you?

STAN   In a house with walls like this, you know everything.

JACK   Well, I'll tell you something else. Not only do these walls have ears, the walls on the house next door have them, and the house next to that one have them ... The whole damn neighborhood has them ... In a community like this, everybody knows everybody else's business ... So what do you think happens when the people in Brighton Beach hear a radio program with a woman on it who sounds familiar, tell us her husband's in ladies' pajamas—and they know what that means—they understand the innuendo ... when they hear that on the radio, what are they thinking when they know that the two sons of the man in ladies' pajamas wrote the program? ... Heh? ... Tell me what they're thinking.

EUGENE   I know what you're getting at, but I don't think that's what's going to happen.

JACK   Can you promise me that? Can you give a written guarantee? ... The only thing people like better than gossip is hearing filth, and that's what those people heard on the radio tonight.

STAN *(Rising)* What are you talking about? That's crazy.

JACK I will never forgive either one of you for ridiculing me in front of my neighbors, in front of my friends, in front of strangers. You'll never know how many people I called to tell to turn on the program because I was so proud of my two sons. That's a mistake I won't make again.

STAN You may have been proud to *them*, but you never encouraged *us*. If it were up to you, I'd still be selling boys' clothing.

JACK After what I heard tonight, I wish to God you were.

EUGENE Stan, stop it! Cut it out!... I'm sorry you feel this way, Pop. We both are. But I swear, we never thought of you and Mom when we wrote the sketch. We just thought of older couples who lived in this neighborhood, but when it got down on paper, I guess it sounded like the ones we knew best ... It wasn't intentional, I swear.
(STAN *sits in the armchair.* JACK *sits between the two boys, but talks to* STAN)

JACK You know what I thought when I heard it? I swear to God. I thought it was their way of getting back at me for hurting their mother ... Is that so impossible to imagine?

STAN No. Not so impossible.

JACK Ah, maybe we're getting closer to the truth now ... What did she tell you about this woman? Did she tell you what she was like?

STAN   I told you. She never talked to me about any of it.

JACK   But you seem to have feelings about it. Where did you get them from? Someone you know from New York? You have lots of friends there, right? Because let me tell you something . . . No matter what you heard about this woman, you will never find a kinder or more decent human being on this earth. You understand me?

STAN   Go to hell.

JACK   What did you say to me?

STAN   I said, "Go to hell!"

EUGENE   Stan. Please. Don't do this.

STAN *(Standing)*   I don't care if she's Joan of Arc, that's still my mother we're talking about. Do whatever you goddamn please, but don't blame Gene and me of humiliating you when you're the one who's been humiliating *us* . . . You're so damn guilty for what you've done, you're accusing everyone else of betraying *you* . . . I never wanted to hear what was happening to you and Mom. I prayed every night you would both work it out and it would pass out of our lives. You could have called each other "him" and "her" forever as long as it kept you together . . . All my life you taught me about things like dignity and principles, and I believed them. I still do, I guess . . . But what kind of principles does a man have when he tells his sons the woman he's seeing on the side is a wonderful, decent human being?

JACK *(Stands, composes himself, then walks slowly to* STAN*)*   Either you've grown up too fast . . . or I've outlived my place in this house.

(JACK *looks at both boys, then goes up the stairs to his bedroom and closes the door*)

EUGENE *(Begins to fold the afghan)* Jesus! I don't believe what just happened . . . I'm shaking, I swear to God.

STAN Do you think what I said was wrong?

EUGENE No. I just don't know if you should have said it.

STAN I didn't bring the subject up, did I? I never accused him of anything. Every one of my friends' fathers screwed around *some* times. Maybe *all* the time. But they don't ask their sons to take the woman into the family.

EUGENE He didn't say it like that.

STAN Screw you, Eugene. What are you taking *his* side for? What are you going to do, buy her a Mother's Day present?

EUGENE I'm not taking his side. Something's happened to him these last few years, I know that. But you don't know his side. You don't know the whole story.

STAN He didn't listen to one word we wrote on that program. He's so paranoid, he thinks it was all about him. Jesus, the one night in our life we wanted his approval, and all he does is tell us what shits we are . . . "Maybe I've outlived this house," he says . . . Is that our fault, too? Another truckload of guilt dumped at our feet . . . He can have the goddamn house because I'm getting out. The both of us. *(He goes to sit beside* EUGENE *on the sofa)* It's time to move, Gene. This is no place for us. We've been waiting for a chance to leave, this is it. They liked our work at CBS, we can afford a place in New

York. We should go, Gene, and we should go soon. (EUGENE *stares at him*) If you don't come, I'll go alone.

EUGENE   No. You're right. I think we should go . . . I just wish it didn't have to be when everything's so bad here.

STAN   There's two or three places I saw. One over on the West Side, with a little backyard that gets the sun. Great place for parties. It'll be better for us, Eug. You'll be able to see your girl friend more often. You'll have your own room, she'll be able to stay overnight.

EUGENE   No. She's not that kind.

STAN   Well, you can bring over the kind that do and take your girl friend to the movies.
     (STAN *goes to straighten the armchair*)

EUGENE   Stan? . . . When we were writing the sketch, did you think we were writing about Mom and Pop?

STAN *(Coming back to sit next to* EUGENE*)*   No. It was like you said. It's everybody out here. I thought the father was Mr. Greenblatt . . . Joe Pinotti's grandfather once fell asleep in his oatmeal. He almost suffocated.

EUGENE   I did. I thought it was Mom and Pop. And Grandpa. They were the ones I was writing about.

STAN   Okay. So? It was a little bit of them, too.

EUGENE   No. It was only them. The joke about him being in ladies' pajamas . . . I didn't mean it the way he said. To me it was just a joke. But maybe I did it subconsciously, the way Pop said.

STAN   If it's subconscious, it's not a crime, Eugene.

EUGENE   I was the one who should have had the fight with him. Only I didn't know I was so angry. Like there's part of my head that makes me this nice, likable, funny kid . . . and there's the other part, the part that writes, that's an angry, hostile real son of a bitch.
   (The phone rings)

STAN *(Going to answer the phone)*   Well, you'd better make friends with the son of a bitch, because he's the one who's going to make you a big living. *(Into the phone)* Hello? . . . Joe? . . . Did you hear it? What'd you think? . . . Wait a minute, I have to tell Gene. *(Turning to* EUGENE*)* Joe Pinotti still can't stop laughing. He thought it was better than Jack Benny. *(Back into the phone)* What? You're kidding . . . Wait a minute . . . *(To* EUGENE*)* His mother and father thought it was about them. They said it was so typical. They loved it. *(Back into the phone)* What? . . . No, they were crazy about it here . . . Yeah, my father thought it was great.
   *(*KATE *enters through the back door, carrying a jar of honey)*

KATE *(Going to the closet to hang up her coat)*   Who's that on the phone?

EUGENE   Joe Pinotti, Stan's friend. He loved the show.

KATE   Why shouldn't he? . . . Where's your father?

EUGENE   Up in his room . . . *your* room.

KATE *(Picking up the tray of sandwiches from the dining table)*   The program's over. You shouldn't be downstairs. Get back in bed.

EUGENE Mom, I'm not eight years old.

KATE You are until you move out of this house.
(She exits into the kitchen)

STAN *(Into the phone)* Can I quote you on that? . . . I'll
talk to you tomorrow, Joe. Yeah . . . Thanks a lot.
(He hangs up the phone) The man sells kitchenware at
Abraham and Straus. He should be the critic on *The
New York Times.*

KATE *(Entering from the kitchen)* What did your father
think of the show?

EUGENE *(Crossing to the stairs)* He thought it was very
lifelike.

STAN He'll probably tell you later.

KATE He tells me hello and goodbye, that's what he
tells me. Hurry up and get dressed. Don't keep a girl
waiting.
*(KATE exits into the kitchen with a tray of cups and
saucers. EUGENE and STAN go into EUGENE's room)*

STAN I don't get it. How can they sleep in the same
bed night after night for a month and not say a word
to each other?

EUGENE I wonder if they say *Gesundheit* if the other
one sneezes.

STAN Jerry Applebaum told me his mother and father didn't talk to each other for over a year, and
they still made love three times a week.
(STAN goes into his own room)

EUGENE That's more times than most people who
talk to each other. *(STAN dresses for his date. EUGENE
turns to the audience)* If I ever married Josie, that

would never happen to us. How could I sleep in the same bed with her without touching her skin and stroking her hair and telling her how much I love her? Then again, maybe that's what my father said before he married my mother.

STAN *(Coming into* EUGENE's *room)* How do I look?

EUGENE Like a Jewish Cary Grant.
(The phone rings)

STAN I've been after this girl for six months, but tonight's the night, kid.

EUGENE How do you know?

STAN She loves celebrities. (STAN *goes downstairs as* KATE *comes out of the kitchen to answer the phone)* Get a good night's sleep. We've got a show to write tomorrow morning.

KATE Not if he's still sick. *(She picks up the phone)* Hello? . . . Who's this? . . . Momma? Oh, my God! I didn't recognize you. You sound wonderful . . . you sound younger.

EUGENE *(Comes out of his room and calls from top of the stairs)* Is that Josie?

KATE It's not Josie. Go to bed. *(Back into phone)* No, Momma, it's Eugene.
(STAN kisses KATE on the cheek, and exits through the front door)

EUGENE Ask her if she heard the show.

KATE *(Into phone)* So, did you make any friends? . . . Uh huh . . . Uh huh . . . Uh huh . . . Momma, you don't have to name them all, I'm glad you made friends.

EUGENE Ask her if she heard the show.

KATE Did you hear the radio show? . . . Eugene and Stanley's . . .

EUGENE Did she like it?

KATE *(To* EUGENE*)* She loved it.

EUGENE Really?

KATE *(Into phone)* You know *who?* . . . The Pitkin family in Coney Island?

EUGENE Oh, my God!

KATE No, Momma. They're actors . . . He's not a dentist. That's a different family . . . These are *actors* . . . All right, Momma. I won't argue with you. If you know them, you know them. *(She shrugs to* EUGENE*)* Yes. Everyone else is fine . . . Jack is doing very well . . . Blanche told you what? . . . No, no. That was months ago. Well, I'm telling you different . . . It's fine . . . *(Looks at* EUGENE, *who is sitting on the steps)* What are you sitting there for? I told you to get to bed. *(He moves slowly up the steps, then stops to listen)* . . . Yes. I know you haven't heard from Poppa . . . He's been very busy. He asks for you all the time . . . No. In his room.

EUGENE You want me to get him?

KATE *(Waving at him to keep quiet)* Momma, let it alone . . . I don't think it's a good idea . . . When he's ready to call you, he'll call you . . . I don't think he means to hurt you. He just has to do things in his own way . . . Listen, you told me once yourself. Men are peculiar . . . I'm not defending him, Momma . . . Where am I taking his side? . . . I told him not to go to Florida? . . . Who told you that? . . . *Who told you that?* . . . I'm not yelling at you, but don't accuse me of what you make up in your own head . . . I didn't say—all right. I'm sorry . . . I said I'm sorry . . . All right, Momma . . . Yes . . . Yes . . . I know you do . . . I do too . . . Goodbye, Momma . . . I'll call you next—

> *(But Momma's clicked off.* KATE *stands there with the phone in her hand. Then replaces it, wiping the receiver clean. She crosses to the breakfront and puts away the flatware.* EUGENE *watches her)*

EUGENE   How about if I made you one of my famous chocolate milkshakes?

KATE   You put too much Hershey's in it. I don't like it so sweet.

EUGENE *(Coming downstairs, to* KATE*)*   You know what I thought?

KATE   What?

EUGENE   I thought when you grew up, you stopped having trouble with your parents.

KATE   Yeah? Then be thankful you're still young.
> *(She goes into the kitchen.* EUGENE *thinks about this for a moment, then looks in at* KATE *in the kitchen)*

EUGENE   I never see you stop working. When Stanley and I make enough money, we're going to get you a maid, Ma.

KATE   A maid? In Brighton Beach? People would pay admission to come over and look at her. *(*EUGENE *sits on the corner of the dining table.* KATE *comes out of the kitchen with a cup of tea)* Oh, my God! Get off that table! *(She whacks him with a dish towel)* Are you crazy, sitting on my dining room table?

EUGENE *(Jumping off the table)* I'm sorry. I didn't leave any marks.

KATE Marks I can clean off. But I never want to see you show disrespect to this table.

EUGENE I didn't mean it . . . I'm sorry, table. I apologize. *(She glares at him)* Is it so expensive?

KATE My grandfather made this table. With his own hands. For my grandmother . . . *(She stirs honey into the tea, then motions for him to sit and drink it)* Over fifty-two years she had this table . . . When I was a little girl, I'd go to her house and she'd let me help her polish it . . . I didn't know it was work. I thought it was fun . . . Maybe because she and I did it together . . . I was closer to her than I was to my own mother . . . Is that a terrible thing to say?

EUGENE Not if that's how you felt.

KATE *(Clearing fruit, candlestick and doilies from the table)* When she died, she left a will. She gave away jewelry, dresses, even a little cash. But she knew what I wanted. *(She looks at the table)* The table you eat on means everything. It's the one time in the day the whole family is together . . . This is where you share things . . . People who eat out all the time don't get to be a family . . . *(She sits at the table)* When I'm gone, if you and your Josie get married, this will be your table.

EUGENE What about Stanley?

KATE Stanley won't get married so fast. And when he does, you make sure he brings his family to eat at your house.

EUGENE Maybe you'll let me polish it with you one day.

KATE   When your wife has a little girl, send *her* over. She and I will polish it.
> *(She collects* EUGENE*'s teacup, and goes into the kitchen)*

EUGENE *(Calling into the kitchen)*   Maybe we'll have twins. You can polish it twice as fast.
> *(*KATE *reenters with furniture polish and a rag. She begins to wipe off the table, with* EUGENE *following closely)*

KATE   Don't follow me around like that. You make me nervous.

EUGENE *(Retreating to the breakfront)*   I'm not following you. I just feel like talking to you . . . I love it when you tell me about the old days.

KATE   I don't remember them anymore. They were such a long time ago.

EUGENE   You just told me about the dining room table, and *that* was a long time ago . . . What was your grandmother like?

KATE *(Stops wiping the table for a moment)*   Tiny. Little bit of a thing. All the women were small in those days. When I was nine years old, I was bigger than she was . . . My grandfather had to pick her up to see the Statue of Liberty.

EUGENE   That must have been some day.

KATE   This is what they dreamed of. Their whole life. To get to America. And when they saw that statue, they started to cry. The women were wailing, the men were shaking, everybody praying. You know why?

EUGENE   Because they were free.

KATE   Because they took one look at that statue and said, "That's not a Jewish woman. We're going to have problems again."

(*She goes back to polishing the table*)

EUGENE   That would be a riot. A Jewish Statue of Liberty. In her left hand, she'd be holding a baking pan . . . and in the right hand, held up high, the electric bill.

KATE   And my grandfather, of course, was a socialist. When *he* saw the statue he said, "It's too big. They should have made a small one and given the money to people who needed it."

EUGENE   If your whole family were socialists, Ma, how come you're not?

KATE   Not the whole family. Just the men . . . A man doesn't fight for political causes on an empty stomach.

EUGENE   But you vote. You voted for President Roosevelt.

KATE   I liked his face. I trusted him. I got nervous that he smoked with a cigarette holder, that was a little fancy for me . . . But he had polio. And I figured a man who walked with crutches wasn't out to take advantage of poor people.

EUGENE   You amaze me sometimes.

KATE   And I like Harry Truman. Him I trust, too.

EUGENE   Why?

KATE   Because he walks everywhere. Seven o'clock in the morning, he's out walking the streets. The Secret Service men can't even keep up with him . . .

He was once a haberdasher, did you know that? And a man who has to get up early in the morning in the winter to open up a store knows what it's like to be a working man . . . All right. That's enough already. I want you in bed.

(She has finished polishing and takes the rag and bottle into the kitchen)

EUGENE   I will. In a few minutes. First tell me about George Raft.

KATE *(Coming out of the kitchen)*   George Raft . . . If I tell you about George Raft again, you're going to tell me you still don't believe me.

(She takes the fruit bowl into the kitchen)

EUGENE   I believe you. I believe every word you say. So tell me how you met George Raft.

KATE *(From the kitchen)*   You heard it a hundred times.

EUGENE *(Putting the skein of yarn around his hands)*   I know. But every time you tell it, it gets a little better. *(She enters from the kitchen, and sees him with the yarn. He pushes the ball of yarn toward her)* Go on.

KATE *(Slowly taking up the ball of yarn and beginning to wind it)*   The night I danced with him, I committed a sin. I knew God was going to punish me for it, and He did. You pay for your mistakes in this world.

EUGENE   What sin did you commit?

KATE   The day before I was going to the Primrose, my Aunt Sipra died. My mother's sister. The next morning, the whole family went to the funeral. I took the day off from work, and that night we all sat at my grandmother's to sit in mourning . . . But I knew that night George Raft was coming to the

Primrose. He was a friend of the owners and he promised he would come. I never dreamed he'd dance with me. I just wanted to watch him. But in the back of my head I thought, if he sees me dance, who knows, he might ask me to get up on the floor with him . . . He wasn't even an actor yet. Just this skinny kid who looked like Rudolph Valentino. But the best ballroom dancer in New York. And to dance with him made you queen of the city.

EUGENE Did he flip a coin like he does in the movies?

KATE Never. But he always smoothed down his hair with his right hand. Every two minutes, smoothing his hair down. It got so shiny, you could see your face in it when you danced with him.

EUGENE So you went to the dance that night.

KATE *(Forgetting the yarn and sitting)* I told my mother I wasn't feeling well. I told her I just threw up in the bathroom, which I didn't, so she sent me home. I knew she and Poppa and the girls wouldn't be home till midnight. So I ran home and changed my dress and went to the Primrose with my girl friend Adele Abrams. And all the time I knew that God was going to punish me for this . . . I kept saying to Adele on the way over, I wish I was a Catholic. Then I could go to church, confess my sins, and God would forgive me. But I knew I just committed another sin by wishing I was Catholic . . . I was throwing my whole life away for this one night to see George Raft.

EUGENE Did you have a—you know—a crush on him?

KATE On George Raft? You think I'm crazy? He was Italian. I was in enough trouble already. He wasn't my type anyway . . . Your father was the one I had the crush on . . . Since I was thirteen years old. He was five years older than me. He went with a whole other crowd. In those days, young people didn't tell each other they had crushes on them. You had to guess. So you sent messages with your eyes, your face, the way you walked by them.

EUGENE   How did you walk by him?

KATE   Not too much, not too little. But he was hard to figure out. He was never a show-off, never a fancy Dan. He didn't smile a lot, but when he did, you knew he meant it. Most boys then smiled at everything. They thought it gave them a good personality. Jack was too honest to put on a good personality. He was what he was . . . and to get a smile from Jack Jerome, you knew you had to earn it . . . But it cost him plenty. The smilers got to be the salesmen. The smilers got to be the bosses. The smilers got all the girls. Your father paid the price for not being a phony . . . It was so hard to impress him. That's why I went to the Primrose that night. I thought if Jack heard that I danced with George Raft, maybe I'd get him to notice me.

EUGENE   This is a movie. There's a whole movie in this story, Ma. And one day I'm going to write it.

KATE   So that night, in a pouring rain, me and Adele Abrams went to the Primrose. My hair got soaking wet, I lost my curls, I wanted to die. But then I got this brilliant idea. Instead of drying it, I combed it straight down and left it wet. Jet black hair. I looked like a Latin from Manhattan . . . The perfect partner for George Raft . . . When I walked out of the ladies' room, my own friends didn't recognize me.

EUGENE   I can't believe this is *my mother* you're talking about.

.KATE   Don't worry. I knew God was going to punish me for the wet hair, too . . . Ten boys must have asked me to dance. But I said no to all of them because I didn't want to tire myself out . . . And then I started to get scared. Because it was ten after eleven and he still didn't show up. If I wasn't home by twelve, my parents would walk in and find out I was lying to them. And with my mother, I didn't need God to punish me.

EUGENE   Twelve o'clock! Cinderella! This story has everything.

KATE   And then, at twenty after eleven, he walks in . . . Like the king of Spain. My heart was beating louder than the drummer in the band . . . He had two friends with him, one on each side, like bodyguards. And I swear, there was something in their inside pockets. I thought to myself, they're either guns or more jars of grease for his hair.

EUGENE   *(To audience)*   She actually had a sense of humor. This was a side of my mother I hardly ever saw. *(To KATE)* So, he walks in with these two guys.

KATE   *(Taking off her sweater and standing center)*   So, he walks in with these two friends and I know I don't have much time. So I grabbed Bobby Zugetti, a shoe clerk, who was the best dancer at the Primrose, and said, "Bobby, dance with me!" . . . I knew he had a crush on me and I never gave him a tumble before. He didn't know what hit him. So out on the floor we go, and we fox-trotted from one side of the ballroom and back. In and out, bobbing and weaving through the crowd, gliding across the floor like a pair of ice skaters.

EUGENE   "Begin the Beguine" . . . Maybe "Night and Day." That's what I would use in the picture.

KATE   And I never once looked over to see if George Raft was looking at me . . . I wanted to get *his* attention, I didn't want to give him mine . . . The music finishes and Bobby dips me down to the floor. It was a little lower than a nice girl should dip, but I figured one more sin wouldn't kill me . . . And I walk over to Adele, I'm dripping with perspiration, and I said, "Well? Did he watch me?" . . . And she said, "It's hard to tell. His eyes don't move." . . . So I look over and he's sitting at a table with his two friends and Adele is right. His eyes don't move. And it's twenty-five to twelve, and he's never even noticed me. And I said to myself, "Well, if it's not meant to be, it's not meant to be." . . . and Adele and I started for the door.

EUGENE   The tension mounts. The audience is on the edge of their seats.

KATE   And as we pass their table, George Raft stands up and says, "Excuse me." And he's looking right at Adele Abrams. He says, "Could I ask you a question, please?" . . . Adele is shaking like a leaf. And she walks over to him.

EUGENE   Adele? He's talking to Adele Abrams?

KATE   And he says, "I wonder if your friend would care to dance with me?" . . . And she says, "You want *me* to ask her?" . . . And he says, "Please. I'm a little shy."

EUGENE   I don't believe it. I don't believe George Raft said that.

KATE   I swear to God. May I never live to see another day.

EUGENE   Even if it's true, it's out of the picture. An audience would never believe it.

KATE   Fine. So Adele says, "I'll ask her." . . . So she comes back and asks me . . . And I look at him and he smiles at me . . . And his eyes moved for the first time. Not fresh or anything, but he had the look of a man with a lot of confidence and I never saw that before. Scared the life out of me. So I walk over to him and he takes my hand and leads me out to the floor . . . Everyone in the Primrose is watching. Even the band. Someone had to whisper, "Start playing," so they would begin . . . And they began. And we danced around that room. And I held my head high and my back straight as a board . . . And I looked down at the floor and up at the ceiling, but never in his eyes. I saw a professional do that once . . . His hands were so gentle. Hardly touching me at all, but I knew exactly when he wanted me to move and which way he wanted me to turn.

EUGENE   *(Dropping the knitting and rushing to the radio)*   Wait a minute! Wait a minute!

KATE   What are you doing?

EUGENE   I want you to show me how you danced.
      (He turns on the radio and begins to search for appropriate music)

KATE   *(Sitting down at the table)*   Show you how I danced thirty-five years ago? I don't even *walk* like I did thirty-five years ago.

EUGENE   Come on. You dance every year with Pop at the Garment Industry Affair. Just show me how you danced with George Raft.

KATE   They danced differently in those days. They don't even do those steps anymore.

EUGENE   Not a whole dance. Two steps . . . One turn . . . *(He finds the right music. It is Benny Goodman's recording of "It Had To Be You")* There! Listen! That's the perfect music . . . *(He crosses to* KATE *at the table)* So he moved you gently around the floor.

KATE   Stop it, Eugene. I'm not in the mood.

EUGENE   *(Holding out his arms to her)*   Come on. I'll dance with you . . . I'm George Raft . . . *(He mimes slicking down his hair)* Everybody is watching us . . . Don't let 'em down, Mom.
     *(*KATE *looks at* EUGENE *for a moment, listening to the music. Then she slowly stands and they begin to dance—awkwardly at first, then more gracefully)*

KATE   You're holding me too tight . . . Don't push me . . . Just with your fingertips.

EUGENE   You're so graceful, Mom . . . I never knew you were so graceful. There's Adele Abrams. *(He waves)* Adele? She's wonderful.
     (They continue to dance)

KATE   Now turn me.

EUGENE   How?

KATE   Just let go. *(He lets go. She does a turn)* Now give me your hand. *(She is back in his arms for the finish of the number)* And then it was over.
     *(*EUGENE *turns off the radio.* KATE *is embarrassed, but flushed with excitement. He smiles at her)*

EUGENE   And then what did he say to you?

KATE   He said, "Thank you. It was my pleasure." And he walked away.

EUGENE   He didn't even ask for your name?

KATE   I didn't ask for his, why should he ask for mine? *(She sits at the dining table)* My God, I'm drenched in perspiration. In the middle of the winter. I don't know how I let you get me to do such things.

EUGENE *(Sitting on the sofa arm, opposite* KATE*)*   Because you liked it. Why do you always stop doing the things that make you feel good?

KATE   What's the matter? Raising you and Stanley wasn't something that made me feel good?

EUGENE   There's other things besides raising a family, Ma.

KATE   Yeah. So I've heard . . . All right. I want you in bed. And no more back talk.
        (She collects the yarn and puts it away)

EUGENE   You didn't finish the story. Did you get home before twelve?

KATE   No. The trolleys were running late. I came in almost twelve-thirty.

EUGENE   And what did your mom and pop say?

KATE   They didn't know. They decided to sleep over at her sister's house. Only Aunt Blanche came home. And she was fast asleep. I didn't tell anybody what I did . . . But in two days, the news was all over the neighborhood. People were congratulating my mother. They treated her like her daughter was a movie star. She was angry with me, but she knew she couldn't say anything . . . But when I saw my grandmother, she winked at me, squeezed my hand, and said, "I know, darling. I know." (*She turns off the dining room lights*) So now do you believe I danced with George Raft?

EUGENE   Yeah. I believe you.

KATE (*Going up the stairs*)   God, I'm exhausted . . . Never ask me that question again. Telling the story was harder than dancing with him.

EUGENE (*Following her up the stairs*)   I think what you did that night was great . . . And you didn't get caught. So God didn't punish you. The movie has a happy ending.

KATE (*Standing at her bedroom door*)   . . . The movie isn't over yet.

EUGENE (*Going into his bedroom and closing the door. To audience*)   I'll be honest about one thing. Dancing with my mother was very scary. I was doing what my father should have been doing with her but wasn't. And holding her like that and seeing her smile was too intimate for me to enjoy. Intimacy is a complex thing. You had to be careful who you shared it with . . . but without it, life was just breakfast, lunch, dinner, and a good night's sleep. Most people would settle for that. Most people do . . . I was determined not to be most people.

(*He leaves his bedroom and goes into the bathroom.*

A lighting change shows us that the night has passed and the sun is coming up. It is early morning the next day.

JACK, *all dressed, comes out of his room. He tiptoes down the stairs, crosses to the back porch, and brings out a large suitcase. He brings it into the living room.*

BEN, *dressed, comes out of his room and down the steps. He stops when he sees* JACK)

BEN Since when do you work on Sundays, Jack?

JACK I didn't expect to see you up so early. I'm sorry, Ben. I haven't got time to talk.

BEN *(Coming into the living room)* Then take the time. Where are you going, Jack?

JACK I'm leaving, Ben. I'm moving out.

BEN I see . . . Did you explain this to Kate?

JACK I thought I'd call her in a few days. I'd say all the wrong things now.

BEN You mean in a few days you'll say all the right things? (JACK *goes to the closet for his coat)* When did you pack your bag?

JACK Friday night . . . when she was out shopping.

BEN You should have told her, Jack. You could have saved money on food for the week.

JACK *(Coming back to his suitcase, coat on)* I've got to leave before she gets up.

BEN So who tells her? Me? If you want me to tell her, you'd better pay me. And I get top money for telling my daughter her husband walked out on her.

JACK This isn't just happening, Ben. This has been coming for a long time. She may be angry when I leave, but she won't be surprised.

BEN You think she'll be angry? . . . You walk out on her after thirty-three years of marriage and you think all she'll be is *angry??* . . . If that's how much you understand her, then maybe she's better off without you.

JACK What do you know about it? For thirty-three years you were a visitor in this house. You came, you ate dinner, and you went home. You didn't live in that bedroom with us ... No matter what anyone tells you, what happens to a man and wife happens in the privacy of that room ... and not even God Himself is there all the time to listen.

BEN You're making a mistake, Jack. No matter what she says, she'll never leave you ... This thing with the other woman won't last ... I know, because I've had enough other women in my life ... Kate will find a way to deal with it. She'll ignore it, she'll pretend it's not happening. She'll live with you and not talk to you to protect her dignity, but she won't leave you ... I'm her own father and I'm saying to you, *have* your affair until it's over, but don't break up what'll last you the rest of your life.

JACK You don't understand. It's not an affair. I don't sleep with this woman. I did once, not now ... She's sick. She'll live another five, six more months. Maybe not even that.

BEN *(Nods)* Maybe to you that's a noble gesture, but to me it stinks.

JACK Don't be so goddamn hypocritical. You've got a seventy-two-year-old wife living alone in Florida, and you stay here pretending you're martyring yourself for a political cause that you haven't been interested in for the last twenty years. I'm the last one to blame you ... Where is it written that a man must love the same woman until the day he dies?

BEN In the marriage vow he took.

JACK If I took it, then you took it too, Ben.

BEN True. And maybe I don't love anymore. Maybe
I am a hypocrite. I don't have another woman, no
. . . My mistress is my privacy. I am unfaithful with
a room upstairs that lets me do what I want. I'm
having an affair with peace and quiet . . . But you're
right. I'm no better than you.

JACK *(At the front door with his suitcase)* I'm fifty-five
years old, Ben. I'm not ready for a room yet. I need
to run. I need to get away from myself and everything I was. I have no more children to raise. I have
nothing waiting out there for me except one thing
. . . Something else!
    (JACK starts to go out the front door)

BEN I still think you're making a mistake, Jack. A big,
big mistake.

JACK *(Turning back)* Why?

BEN . . . Because Kate is my daughter.

JACK I'll call the boys tomorrow.
    (JACK goes.
        *BEN sits on the sofa, then hears KATE coming out of
    her bedroom. He hurries into the kitchen.*
        *KATE comes out in a housedress, goes downstairs
    and looks out the front door window for a moment.*
        *BEN comes out of the kitchen with a roll on a plate
    with butter on the side and a knife)*

BEN How long have you been up?

KATE A few minutes. I heard Jack coming downstairs, I thought he must be hungry. Did you put up
hot water?

BEN *(Sitting at the table)* Certainly I put up hot water. What am I, an invalid?
  (He butters his roll)

KATE You want some eggs?

BEN No.

KATE *(Crossing to the back porch)* No eggs?

BEN Why do you always ask me if I want eggs? If I wanted eggs, wouldn't I ask you?

KATE It's too early in the morning, Poppa. Don't start in.

BEN Listen, if it'll make you happy to make me eggs, make them. Scrambled, not too loose.

KATE You just said you didn't want any.

BEN I don't. I'm having them for you.

KATE *(Angrily)* Don't ask me to make you things if you don't want them. *(She catches herself)* I'm sorry. I hardly slept last night.

BEN I heard the music. I heard you dancing with Eugene. I forgot all about your grandmother giving you the dining room table.

KATE You forget a lot of things. Poppa. You shouldn't have been listening.

BEN I know. But I enjoyed it. I left my door open a crack ... Some boys you got, Kate. You raised them good, believe me.

KATE Where is Jack so long? Is he in the kitchen? No one lets me cook here anymore. *(She goes into the kitchen.* BEN *stares at his roll.* KATE *comes back to the table)* Is he in the house?

BEN No.

KATE Where'd he go, for a walk?

BEN No.

KATE He's not in the house and he didn't go for a walk . . . So where'd he go on a Sunday morning? *(She looks at* BEN, *who hasn't moved. And suddenly she realizes . . . She turns away)* Why didn't you tell me? . . . You think I wasn't expecting it?

BEN I didn't know how to say it . . . He's gone, Kate . . . He moved out . . . It's as simple as that.
(She stands there a moment, not saying a word. Then she goes out to the porch, lights a cigarette, and looks out.

BEN *goes into the kitchen.*

EUGENE *comes out of the bathroom, fully dressed. His cold is gone. Time is in transition. He stands at the top of the stairs)*

EUGENE *(To audience)* When Mom heard the news about Pop, she didn't cry, she didn't reach for anyone to hug, she didn't make a sound . . . When I was in the army, they told us, in battle, don't bother attending the wounded who were crying for help . . . Go to those who didn't make a sound. They were the ones in real trouble . . . (KATE *finishes her cigarette and goes into the kitchen.* EUGENE *comes down the stairs into the living room. To audience)* . . . The winter moved on and so did our careers. As the temperature grew colder, Stan and I got hotter. They doubled our salary at CBS and we were washing our hands in the same john as Arthur Godfrey . . .
*(*STAN *comes running excitedly down the street and into the house. He sees* EUGENE)*

STAN Okay. Don't say a word. Just sit down.

EUGENE What?

STAN Will you just sit down. Because you're not
going to believe this. Go on. *(EUGENE sits)* No. Stand
up. This news is too important to be sitting.

EUGENE *(Getting up again)* What are you talking
about?

STAN Where's Mom? . . . *Mom!!* Come on inside.
Grandpa? . . . Where's Grandpa?

EUGENE He fell asleep on the kitchen table.
*(KATE comes in from the kitchen and stands by the
breakfront, looking at the two boys)*

STAN Mom! . . . Remember I once told you, you have
to have faith in me . . . I knew talent when I see it
and I knew right away that Eugene and I had it
. . . I never gave up on us, did I? . . . Did I, Eugene?

EUGENE No. Never . . . Except for the eight times you
wanted to commit suicide.

STAN *(Hanging up his coat)* Except for those eight
times, I was like a rock.

EUGENE And once you smashed the typewriter with
my baseball bat.

STAN Except for the time I smashed the typewriter,
I never lost heart, right?

EUGENE Except for the time you lost heart.

STAN But otherwise, I never faltered. Never gave up
hope. So guess what I'm going to tell you?

EUGENE You gave up hope.

STAN We got "The Phil Silvers Show." You, me, and two other writers . . . Two hundred dollars a week . . . Apiece . . . *APIECE!!* . . . That's four hundred dollars a week . . . Do you realize how much money that is?

EUGENE *Three* hundred dollars a week?

STAN *(Hugging* EUGENE*)* Congratulate me, you lousy kid. I negotiated the whole deal myself. We don't even have to pay an agent.

EUGENE You're incredible . . . When do we start?

STAN Three weeks from Monday. They wanted to know if we thought we could double on "The Chubby Waters Show," but I turned them down. It's too much work.

EUGENE We can handle it. Why don't we do it?

STAN No! Big mistake. We spread ourselves too thin, we'll lose the quality. If we make good here, we'll get the big money later . . . So what do you think about this, Mom?

KATE What do I think? . . . I got two geniuses, that's what I think.

STAN *(Kissing* KATE*)* Three geniuses, because you're the one who gave birth to us . . . That's why I think you should be living in New York, too.

KATE New York? What are you talking about?

STAN *(Going to stand beside* EUGENE*)* Gene and I are moving next week . . . I signed the lease today. We'll be working night and day, it would be murder for us to come out *here* to visit you. The woman showed me a place two blocks away. Perfect for you and Grandpa. Before you say no, come and look at it.

KATE In the first place, if your grandfather didn't go to Miami, he won't go to New York. In the second place, who do I know in the city?

EUGENE Aunt Blanche.

KATE Aunt Blanche lives on Park Avenue. I don't have clothes to visit Park Avenue . . . I have my friends here. I like the stores better. You know what they would charge me for chicken breasts in New York? Forget it.

STAN I just want you to be happy, Mom.

KATE You made me happy enough today. Too much happiness and I get scared.

STAN *(Slapping* EUGENE's *shoulder)* Come on upstairs. We've got things to talk about.
    (EUGENE *goes upstairs ahead of* STAN)

KATE What day are you moving?

STAN Next Monday.

KATE Did you call the movers?

STAN *(On the stairs)* We're not taking any furniture, Mom. We're getting all new stuff. We're just taking our clothes.

KATE You don't want the bureau? It's a beautiful bureau. Your father and I bought that new in Bamberger's.

STAN That was twenty-five years ago, Mom.

KATE You don't want it, don't take it. I'll save it. Maybe your children will want it.

STAN Gene's children. I'm not ready for marriage yet.

KATE   Well, get ready. If I don't get grandchildren, what did I need children for?

(KATE *goes into the kitchen.* STAN *and* EUGENE *go into* EUGENE'*s room*)

STAN *(Closing the door)*   I got other news, too. I saw Pop today. He was waiting for me outside CBS.

EUGENE *(Sitting on the bed)*   No kidding. How is he?

STAN   The lady he was seeing? Audrey? They took her to the hospital yesterday. He said she won't last out the week.

EUGENE   That's too bad. How was Pop taking it?

STAN   He looked lousy. He asked about Mom. He asked if she was all right. Then he started to cry. We were in Louie's Restaurant on Madison Avenue. He grabbed my hand and held it. He sat there for half the lunch holding my hand. The waiter looked at us like we were a couple of lovers.

EUGENE   You think when this Audrey—you know—you think he'll come back to Mom?

STAN   No. I asked him. At least not for now. He said to me, "No, I can't go back to that house . . . Besides, she'd never take me back," he says.

EUGENE   Sure she would. She still loves him.

STAN   Maybe. But she's stubborn. Like Grandpa.

EUGENE   Why are they doing this to each other, Stan?

STAN   I don't know. Maybe he explains it all in the letters.

EUGENE   What letters?

STAN   He gave me two letters. One for me, one for you.

EUGENE What's in it?

STAN *(Handing* EUGENE *a letter)* I don't know.

EUGENE You didn't read yours?

STAN He doesn't want us to. Not yet.

EUGENE When can we read them?

STAN After he dies.

EUGENE After he dies?

STAN He made me promise him that. I said, "If it's important, Pop, why can't you tell us what's in it now?" He said he just couldn't. We would have to wait.

EUGENE Suppose he lives to be ninety? They'll turn yellow, we'll never be able to read it.

STAN They're probably letters of apology. Explaining why he did what he did.

EUGENE By then I'd be fifty-four. I wouldn't even care.

STAN Or maybe the letters say he'll never forgive us for what *we* did. For my saying "go to hell" to him.

EUGENE He already forgave you. He held your hand in the restaurant . . . So? Are you going to wait until he dies to read it?

STAN I'm going to try . . . What about you?

EUGENE Suppose I die before him? Does he get his letter back?

STAN You're funny, Gene. You've got a wonderfully inventive mind, but sometimes it lacks respect.
     *(*STAN *goes into his own room. He looks at his own letter, then puts it in his pocket, takes out a suitcase, and packs.*

EUGENE *turns his envelope over in his hands. Then he looks at the audience)*

EUGENE *(To audience)*   It probably does. I was really confused. I always loved my father, but I didn't like him for leaving my mother and I was really sore at him for leaving me this thing . . . I sure didn't want him to die, but how else would I get to read the damn letter? I knew I was really angry when I thought about sending him a gift on Father's Day and printing on it, "Never Ever To Be Opened" . . . The following Monday was our last day in Brighton Beach. *(He puts on a jacket and puts the letter in the inside pocket. As he speaks, he takes out a suitcase from under the bed and packs.*

(STAN comes out of his room with the suitcase and crosses downstairs. He gets their coats out of the closet)   Stan and I didn't have much to take. We were going to throw out our old clothes, but Mom put them in a box in the basement. Just in case. Daughters of socialists don't have too much faith in show business.

(EUGENE leaves his room and brings his suitcase downstairs. BEN *comes out of the kitchen)*

STAN   Where's Mom?

BEN   In the kitchen baking you two years' worth of cookies.

EUGENE *(Putting on his coat)*   Remember your promise, Gramps. You're going to come to the studio to watch the first show.

BEN   Only if it's about something. If it's just funny, I'm not interested.

EUGENE   No, no. The first show is about a girl from Mount Holyoke. She meets a boy named Myron Trotsky.

STAN *(Sitting on the sofa arm)* Why did you tell him? Now he knows the ending.

BEN You still like to kid me, you two. You think I never knew when you were kidding me? I'll tell you something. When you were kidding me, I was kidding you twice as much.

KATE *(Coming out of the kitchen carrying a large cardboard box tied with string)* Don't jiggle the box too much. It makes crumbs.

EUGENE *(Taking the box)* How much should we ask for them, Mom? We're going to sell them on the train.

STAN No train. We're making *this* trip in a cab.

BEN Don't let my friends see you getting into a cab.

STAN Am I going to get a hug from you, Gramps?

BEN A hug yet. You really want to humiliate me, don't you?

STAN No. I just want to say goodbye.
(STAN *hugs* BEN *and kisses his cheek, then steps away)*

BEN *(To* EUGENE*)* I suppose I'm going to get the same thing from you, heh?

EUGENE Of course. I'm going to kiss you right on the lips. They're going to have to pull us apart.
(EUGENE *hugs* BEN *and kisses his cheek, then steps away)*

STAN *(To* KATE*)* Hey! Broadway Momma! *(Opens his arms)* Step right into these arms.

KATE Yesterday he was a writer, today he's Clark Gable.
(STAN *kisses* KATE *and gives her a long hug. Then he steps away)*

EUGENE I just want to say one thing, Ma . . .

KATE Don't say anything. You know me. I don't deal with these things too good.

EUGENE It's not that horrible. And it's quick . . . I love you. Okay? That wasn't so bad, was it?
(EUGENE *kisses* KATE *and gives her a long hug*)

STAN Okay, come on, let's go! We're not moving to Budapest. We've got a party at four o'clock.
(EUGENE *steps away from* KATE *and goes to his suit-case at the front door*)

EUGENE What party?

STAN At CBS. Do you realize the gorgeous women we're going to meet today.

KATE Stanley! He's got Josie. You leave him alone.
(EUGENE *opens the front door and sets his suitcase outside*)

STAN (*In the open door*) I was kidding, Mom. I won't let a single beautiful showgirl get near him. We'll call you in a few days . . . And, Grandpa, just so you know, I always knew when you were kidding me.

BEN I knew when you knew.
(BEN *and* KATE *exit into the kitchen.* STAN *brings his suitcase outside and stands beside* EUGENE)

STAN Come on. It's freezing.

EUGENE I just want to look at the house for a minute.

STAN I'm going to look for a cab. I don't care what it costs, this is one party I'm not missing . . . I told you we'd make it, didn't I? I picked Joe DiMaggio and us. Not bad, huh?

(He runs up the street to look for a cab)

EUGENE *(To audience)*   I knew then that no matter how many times I came back to see this house, it would never be my home again . . . Mom and Pop split up for good and never got back together . . . As a matter of fact, he remarried about two years later, to a pretty nice woman. Mom would really be hurt if she heard me say that, but the truth is the truth . . . Grandpa found it rough going in his seventy-eighth year and finally surrendered to capitalism and Miami Beach . . . He plays pinochle every day and donates half his winnings to the Socialist Party . . . Josie and I got married and we sleep each night with her hand lying gently across my chest. I won't even breathe for fear she'll move it away.

STAN *(Running down the street to* EUGENE*)*   Gene! Come on! I got a cab!

EUGENE   I'm coming. I'm coming.

STAN   I never realized how cold it was out here before.
   *(*STAN *exits up the street, taking* EUGENE*'s box of cookies with him) (*KATE *comes out and begins to wax her table under Eugene's speech)*

EUGENE *(To audience)*   I didn't keep my promise to Pop. I opened his letter and read it. He didn't apologize, and he wasn't mad at Stan and me for what we wrote. The only thing he wanted was for Stan and me to understand his side of the story . . . Only he never said what his side was . . . Contrary to popular belief, everything in life doesn't come to a clear-cut conclusion. Mom didn't do anything very exciting with the rest of her life except wax her grandmother's table and bask in the joy of her sons' success. But I never got the feeling that Mom felt she sacrificed herself for us. Whatever she gave, she found her own quiet pleasure in. I guess she was never comfortable with words like *I love you.* A hard life can sometimes knock the sentiment out of you . . . But all in all, she considers herself a pretty lucky woman. After all, she did once dance with George Raft.

> (EUGENE *turns away from the house, grabs his suitcase, and runs up the street to the cab)* (KATE *continues waxing the table)*
>
> *Curtain*

ABOUT THE AUTHOR

Since 1960, a Broadway season without a NEIL SIMON comedy or musical has been a rare one. His first play was *Come Blow Your Horn*, followed by the musical *Little Me*. During the 1966–67 season, *Barefoot in the Park*, *The Odd Couple*, *Sweet Charity* and *The Star-Spangled Girl* were all running simultaneously; in the 1970–71 season, Broadway theatergoers had their choice of *Plaza Suite*, *Last of the Red Hot Lovers* and *Promises, Promises*. Next came *The Gingerbread Lady*, *The Prisoner of Second Avenue*, *The Sunshine Boys*, *The Good Doctor*, *God's Favorite*, *California Suite*, *Chapter Two*, *They're Playing Our Song*, *I Ought to Be in Pictures*, *Fools*, a revival of *Little Me*, *Brighton Beach Memoirs*, *Biloxi Blues* (which won the Tony Award for Best Play), the female version of *The Odd Couple* and *Broadway Bound*.

NEIL SIMON began his writing career in television, writing *The Phil Silvers Show* and Sid Caesar's *Your Show of Shows*. Mr. Simon has also written for the screen: the adaptations of *Barefoot in the Park*, *The Odd Couple*, *Plaza Suite*, *The Prisoner of Second Avenue*, *The Sunshine Boys*, *California Suite*, *Chapter Two*, *I Ought to Be in Pictures* and the forthcoming *Brighton Beach Memoirs*. His other screenplays include *The Out-of-Towners*, *The Heartbreak Kid*, *Murder by Death*, *The Goodbye Girl*, *The Cheap Detective*, *Seems Like Old Times*, *Only When I Laugh*, *Max Dugan Returns* and *The Slugger's Wife*.

The author lives in California. He has two daughters, a stepdaughter and a grandson.

OUTSTANDING DRAMA

0452

☐ **FIVE PLAYS BY MICHAEL WELLER.** With unmatched intimacy and accuracy, this remarkable collection of plays captures the feelings, the dilemmas, the stances, and above all the language of the 1980's. This volume brings together for the first time five of Weller's plays, in their author's final versions. (261201—$12.95)

☐ **LORRAINE HANSBERRY, THE COLLECTED LAST PLAYS.** The three plays in this volume represent the fullest unfolding of the remarkable genius that created *A Raisin in the Sun,* and *Sidney Brustein's Window.* These plays are the lasting legacy of the extraordinarily gifted woman whom Julius Lester calls in his Foreword "the ultimate black writer for today . . . My God, how we need her." (254140—$8.95)

☐ **FENCES A Play by August Wilson.** The author of the 1984-85 Broadway season's best play, *Ma Rainey's Black Bottom,* return with another powerful, stunning dramatic work. "Always absorbing . . . the work's protagonist—and greatest creation—is a Vesuvius of rage . . . The play's finest moments perfectly capture that inky almost imperceptibly agitated darkness just before the fences of racism, for a time, came crashing down."—Frank Rich, *The New York Times.* (260485—$6.95)

☐ **MA RAINEY'S BLACK BOTTOM, By August Wilson.** The time is 1927. the place is a run-down recording studio in Chicago where Ma Rainey, the legendary blues singer is due to arrive. What goes down in the session to come is more than music, it is a riveting portrayal of black rage . . . of racism, of the self-hate that racism breeds, and of racial exploitation. (261139—$7.95)

Prices slightly higher in Canada.

PLAYS BY TENNESSEE WILLIAMS
(0451)

☐ **CAT ON A HOT TIN ROOF by Tennessee Williams.** The Pulitzer Prize-winning drama of guilt, frustration and greed set in Mississippi. "Mr. Williams' finest drama. It faces and speaks the truth."—Brooks Atkinson, *The New York Times*
(158695—$3.95)

☐ **A STREETCAR NAMED DESIRE by Tennessee Williams.** This is one of the most remarkable plays of our times. It created an immortal woman in the Character of Blanche DuBois, the haggard and fragile southern beauty whose pathetic last grasp at happiness is cruelly destroyed ... and Stanley Kowalski, a sweat-shirted barbarian, the crudely sensual brother-in-law who precipitates Blanche's tragedy.
(154452—$3.50)

☐ **TENNESSEE WILLIAMS: FOUR PLAYS.** This superb collection includes *Summer and Smoke*, the story of two ill-starred lovers—one hungered for the spirit, the other hungered for the flesh ... *Orpheus Descending*, the searing drama of a wandering guitar player and the storekeeper's wife he loved ... *Suddenly Last Summer*, he was a corrupt pleasure-seeker and she was the beautiful young cousin he had chosen as a victim ... *Period of Adjustment*, they were two young couples fighting love out on the battlefield of marriage. ...
(520157—$4.95)

☐ **THREE BY TENNESSEE by Tennessee Williams.** This volume includes *Sweet Bird of the Youth*, the story of the aging actress and the young stud—two lovers trying to escape their hidden selves ... *The Rose Tattoo*, a lonely Italian widow finds a physician substitute for her husband in virile truckdriver ... *The Night of the Iguana*, a spitfire sensualist and a genteel spinster fight desperately for the affections of a defrocked minister.
(521498—$4.95)

Prices slightly higher in Canada.

There's an epidemic with 27 million victims. And no visible symptoms.

It's an epidemic of people who can't read.

Believe it or not, 27 million Americans are functionally illiterate, about one adult in five.

The solution to this problem is you... when you join the fight against illiteracy. So call the Coalition for Literacy at toll-free **1-800-228-8813** and volunteer.

Volunteer Against Illiteracy. The only degree you need is a degree of caring.